Contents

INTRODUCTION

Smoking represents the single most preventable cause of death in the United Kingdom. Presented here are estimates for 1995 of the number of deaths that could have been delayed. The figure relates to deaths among adults resulting from their own smoking. Deaths over age 35 years only were considered, allowing for the relatively long lead time to deaths caused by smoking, and because this is the age group for whom the data on mortality risks of smoking were available. The effects of passive smoking or smoking in pregnancy are not included. As the extreme health consequence of smoking, the number of deaths provides an indicator of much more widespread effects on quality of life, ranging from general morbidity to chronic debilitating disease.

The report updates the previous Health Education Authority estimate.[1] This figure, 110,000 deaths caused by smoking in 1988, was described at the time as a cautious estimate, to be updated as and when the evidence on diseases caused by smoking became available. The current update was prompted by further evidence about the diseases which can be caused by smoking, by the availability of more complete data on the mortality risks of smoking and by the need to take account of changing mortality implications of the smoking epidemic, especially as women from cohorts which featured highest smoking levels reach ages of highest mortality.

Smoking is a habit acquired early, by young people with more pressing concerns than thoughts of mortality risk in some distant future. They know the risks of smoking but the risks seem remote. Knowing also that risks fall appreciably on quitting, they feel it is safe to smoke for now. They postpone quitting until a more appropriate time in their life, when they do not need it, or when other priorities emerge. Thus they become addicted, unaware of the detrimental effects of their dependency in future whatever their circumstances.

A majority of cigarette smokers routinely say that they would like to give up smoking, and still more of them have tried in the past to quit smoking. The imperative to quit and awareness of their dependency develops among cigarette smokers soon after they start to smoke, becoming a nagging reality in their lives.

Smokers who do not want to give up, as well as many of those who do, defend or rationalise their continuing smoking in a variety of ways. They cite the many other risky behaviours and conflicting expert advice about them to diminish the force of the anti-smoking message. They stress the advantages of smoking in their own lives and highlight environmental and stress-inducing factors over which they have no control as more damaging to their health than smoking. They also postpone quitting, reassured by knowledge of the reduction or reversibility in risk after quitting. Absence of a sense of immediate risk supports this attitude since people who die from their smoking do so many years after their first cigarette.

Smoking is not an immediate cause of death in itself, rather a cause of the disease from which the smoker dies. The lethal cocktail contained in tobacco smoke, including more than 4,000 chemical constituents, many of them toxic, mutagenic and carcinogenic, kills via diseases ranging across the spectrum. Individuals who die from smoking cannot be identified. Smoking status is not included on the death certificate and even if it were it would not be possible to conclude causation in each case. People who have never smoked cigarettes die from diseases that smoking can cause, and to that same extent some cigarette smokers too can die of the disease but not as a result of their smoking. The methods used to estimate the number of deaths caused by smoking are all based on a proportion of deaths caused by smoking, and cannot be traced back to individuals.

Absence of the individual link, the outcome based on risk rather than predetermined and the relatively long time it

1

takes for smoking to kill renders smoking as a cause of death particularly prone to the use of supposed counter-examples. Commonly cited cases of longevity among acquaintances or relatives who had smoked 60 cigarettes a day for years unscathed are used as counter-examples. Few would knowingly place themselves at risk of a potentially fatal infectious disease whose consequences are immediate, even though the risk of death be low and many who have survived unscathed can be cited. The smoking message is clear, that cigarette smoking for substantial numbers of smokers is a time bomb which, though it may take some time to take effect, is guaranteed to kill them prematurely.

The long lead time to death from smoking makes analysis and interpretation of trends in mortality more complex, it being necessary to consider past as well as present smoking behaviour. This is even more so when trends in smoking fluctuate, and when the product itself undergoes changes purported to reduce the damage it can do. People dying now and in the near future made their key smoking decisions on the whole some years ago. The effect on mortality of discouraging young people from smoking would be huge, but would not be fully realised for many decades. The effect of smokers quitting now would be less but would be realised earlier. In either case, immediate health benefits would accrue.

An overview of cigarette smoking in the UK and consequences for today's UK mortality provides the context before the estimates of deaths caused by smoking and consideration of the outlook for the future.

5.00

THE UK SMOKING EPIDEMIC: DEATHS IN 1995

Christine Callum

Acknowledgements

Thanks are due to Richard Doll, Richard Peto and Nicholas
Wald for expert advice and comments; Department of
Health colleagues, Anne Emery for collaborating in
production of the estimates and Patsy Bailey and Helen
Giles for guidance and support throughout the
development of the report; the American Cancer Society
for providing data from the Cancer Prevention II Study; the
Office for National Statistics, General Register Office for
Scotland, General Register Office for Northern Ireland and
Northern Ireland Statistics and Research Agency for
providing data on mortality and smoking; HEA colleagues,
in particular Dean Mahoney, Ann McNeill and Lesley Owen
for support in production of the report.

ISBN 0 7521 1142 6

© Health Education Authority, 1998

Health Education Authority

Trevelyan House

30 Great Peter Street

London

SW1P 2HW

Designed by The John Burke Design Consultancy

Printed in England

CIGARETTE **SMOKING** IN THE UK: THE **PRESENT** SITUATION

Cigarette smoking status

In Great Britain in 1996 an estimated 28% of those aged 16 years or more were cigarette smokers: 29% of men and 28% of women.[2] Cigarette smoking varies according to age, rising to a maximum among men and women in their early 20s and falling thereafter as some of them quit smoking (Figure 2.1). In the age group 16-19, 26% of men and 32% of women were cigarette smokers, rising respectively to 43% and 36% of those aged 20-24 and falling with age thereafter, to around 10% of those aged 75 years or more. Cigarette smoking varies more with age among men than women, a

steeper rise to a higher peak and sharper subsequent fall, and the sex differential in smoking changes accordingly with age. In the youngest age group women were more likely than men to be cigarette smokers, the reverse being the case between ages 20 and 44, and between ages 45 and 74 smoking levels tending to be roughly equal, though higher on balance among women.

Current and ex-cigarette smokers together represent the percentage who have ever smoked cigarettes. (Figure 2.2)

Figure 2.1 **Percentage who smoke cigarettes by sex and age: Great Britain 1996**

■ men
□ women

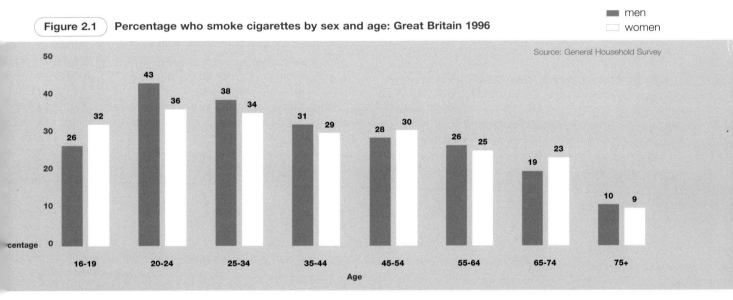

Source: General Household Survey

Figure 2.2 **Percentage who are current and ex-smokers by sex and age: Great Britain 1996**

■ current smokers
□ ex-smokers

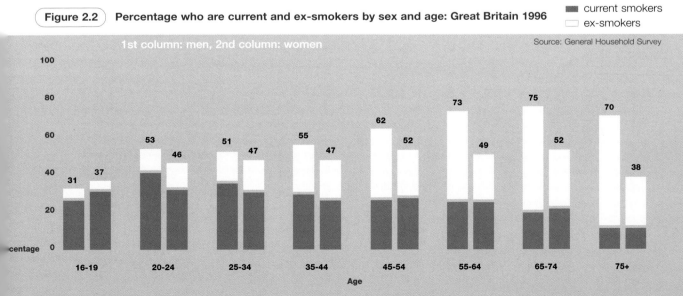

1st column: men, 2nd column: women

Source: General Household Survey

Starting to smoke

In the age group 16-19 women were more likely than men to have ever started smoking. Over 20 years men were more likely than women to have ever smoked cigarettes, increasingly so between ages 35 and 54 and most noticeably among those aged 55 years or more. In age groups 45 years or more there were progressively large percentages of men who were ex-smokers, in fact ex-smokers outnumbered current smokers. This was the case for women only among those aged 65 years or more.

Overall the patterns by age of smoking status are quite distinct for men and women, though in younger age groups a convergence is apparent. (Figure 2.3)

The figures of cigarette smoking status by age reflect two distinct aspects of smoking behaviour, starting to smoke and quitting, presenting distinct public health challenges – discouraging people from taking up smoking and encouraging smokers to quit.

Discouraging people from starting to smoke has to focus on the young, as the smoking habit is acquired early. In England in 1996, more than one in eight (13%) secondary school children aged 11-15 years said that they smoked at least one cigarette a week.[3] Recruitment rises rapidly between ages 11 and 15, and is higher among girls than boys. By age 15, more than one in four (28%) boys and one in three (33%) girls smoked cigarettes in 1996.[4] (Figure 2.4)

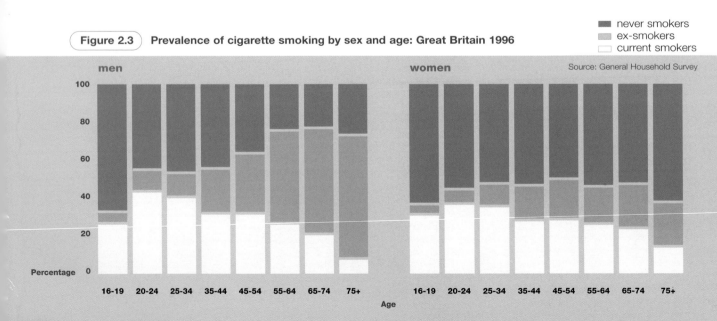

Figure 2.3 **Prevalence of cigarette smoking by sex and age: Great Britain 1996**

never smokers
ex-smokers
current smokers

Source: General Household Survey

men

women

Percentage

16-19 20-24 25-34 35-44 45-54 55-64 65-74 75+

Age

Quitting

Many of those who have ever smoked cigarettes have decided to quit and succeeded in quitting. (Figure 2.5)

The likelihood increases with age. Men aged 35 years or more who had ever been smokers were more likely than women to have quit smoking. In the age group 45-54 years for example 55% of men who had ever smoked had quit

smoking compared with 43% of women. These figures seem to reflect the impact of health education measures targeted at middle and older age men. Between ages 20 and 34 men appeared slightly less likely than women to have quit. However it is possible that quitting levels for women in this age group are inflated by 'temporary' quitting associated with pregnancy and looking after infants and young children.

Figure 2.4   Percentage aged 11-15 who smoke cigarettes by sex and age: England 1996

■ boys
☐ girls

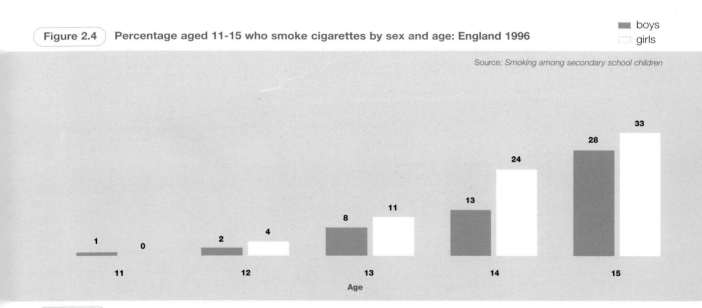

Source: *Smoking among secondary school children*

Figure 2.5   Percentage of those who have ever smoked cigarettes who have quit smoking by sex and age: Great Britain 1996

■ men
☐ women

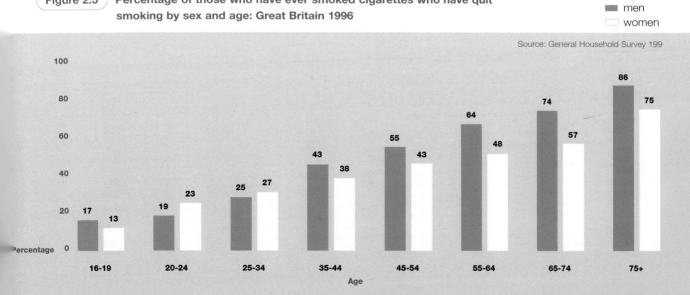

Source: General Household Survey 199

Inclination to quit

The desire to quit smoking follows shortly after recruitment, and displays much less variation with age than actual quitting. (Figure 2.6)

In 1994, even by age 16-24 more than two in three smokers said that they would like to give up smoking altogether. The figure peaks at nearly three in four smokers aged 25-34, but remains high, more than 70%, for men up to age 54 and women up to age 44. Thereafter the figure falls with age, more steeply among men than women. It remains relatively high in older age groups however, around 60% of smokers aged 55-74 years who said that they would like to quit. In the younger age groups women are slightly more likely than men to say they would like to quit, whilst among those aged 45 years or more, with one exception, the reverse applies.

Trying to quit also starts early, two in three smokers aged 16-24 in England in 1996 saying that they had ever tried to quit.[5] (Figure 2.7)

Figure 2.6 **Percentage of smokers who would like to give up smoking cigarettes by sex and age: Great Britain 1994**

■ men
☐ women

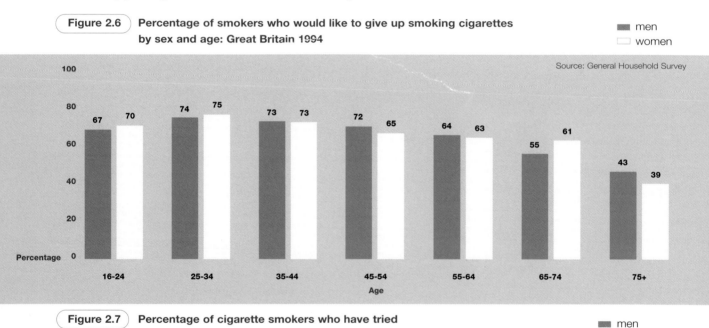

Source: General Household Survey

Figure 2.7 **Percentage of cigarette smokers who have tried to quit smoking cigarettes by sex and age: England 1996**

■ men
☐ women

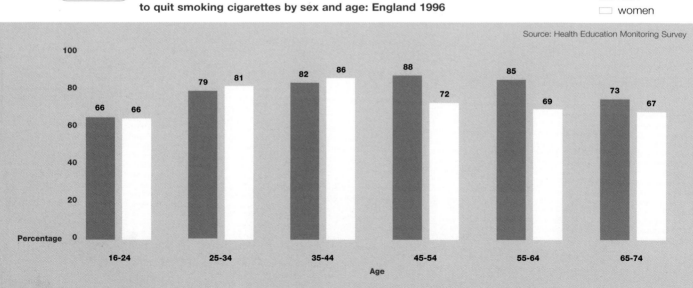

Source: Health Education Monitoring Survey

The figures rise with age, peaking among women aged 35-44 years at 86% and among men aged 45-54 years at 88%. Attempts to quit were a little more common among women than men aged 25-44, above which they were higher among men. The sex differential in trying to quit is consistent with that in succeeding or wanting to quit, higher figures for women than men aged 25-44 years suggesting previous attempts to quit in response to pregnancy. In this case the figure is more likely to include successful attempts to quit for temporary reasons, to be resumed later.

The figures for present desire to quit and past attempts to do so combined demonstrate how widespread the smoking message is, at least in terms of knowledge, articulating and perhaps internalising it, if not its realisation. (Figure 2.8)

Only one in five smokers aged 16-24 years neither wanted, nor had tried, to give up smoking, falling to less than one in ten of those aged 25-34 and one in twenty men aged 45-54 years. Above age 45 years, women were more likely than men neither to have tried nor want to give up smoking, similar to the disparity in actual quitting. Increasing numbers who have tried but do not want to give up among men aged 45 or more are apparent, amounting to 30% of those aged

55-64. This may depict men who had tried to give up in response to initial publicity about the harmful effects of smoking but for whom it had proved too difficult, a resigned attitude replacing the momentum to quit.

High prevalence of present desire and past attempts to quit among current smokers suggests that giving up in many cases is not once-for-all, involving several attempts and with relapse quite common, whether due to difficulties in quitting or because quitting is perceived as short-term, as often the case for women who give up during pregnancy. One in five current cigarette smokers aged 25-74 in England in 1993 for example claimed to have succeeded in giving up in the past for at least a year.[6] The figure is highest among those aged 35-44, 28% of men and 26% of women who currently smoked claiming to have quit in the past for a period of at least a year, and is higher among women than men aged 45 years or more. (Figure 2.9)

The current smoking status figures thus represent a 'net' snapshot of a fluid process, ex-smokers including some who will relapse and start to smoke again and current smokers including some who have given up in the past and will do so again.

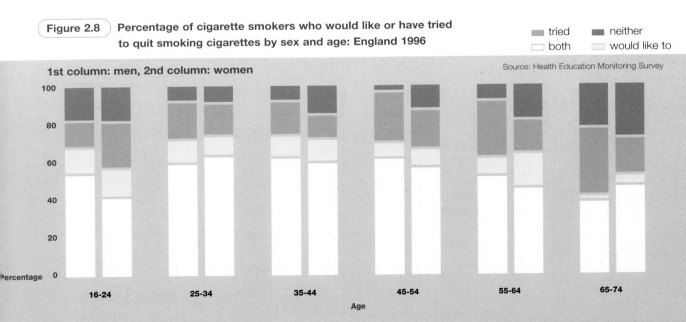

Figure 2.8) Percentage of cigarette smokers who would like or have tried to quit smoking cigarettes by sex and age: England 1996

tried   neither
both   would like to

1st column: men, 2nd column: women

Source: Health Education Monitoring Survey

Percentage

16-24   25-34   35-44   45-54   55-64   65-74

Age

2

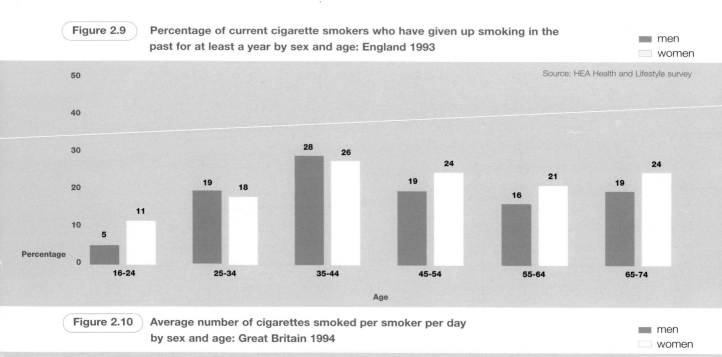

Figure 2.9 — Percentage of current cigarette smokers who have given up smoking in the past for at least a year by sex and age: England 1993

men / women

Source: HEA Health and Lifestyle survey

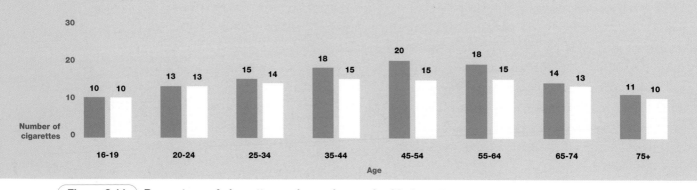

Figure 2.10 — Average number of cigarettes smoked per smoker per day by sex and age: Great Britain 1994

men / women

Source: General Household Survey

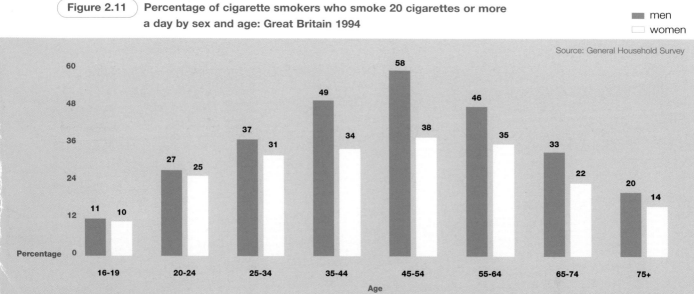

Figure 2.11 — Percentage of cigarette smokers who smoke 20 cigarettes or more a day by sex and age: Great Britain 1994

men / women

Source: General Household Survey

Consumption

The number of cigarettes smoked is higher among men than women who smoke, 16.2 compared with 13.9 cigarettes a day in 1994. Cigarette consumption among men increases with age, peaking at age 45-54 and falling thereafter. (Figure 2.10) Consumption varies less by age among women, though it follows a similar pattern to that in men. A narrow gap in consumption between men and women at age 16-19 widens with age until age 45-54 years, narrowing thereafter.

Measured in terms of the proportion of heavy smokers, the difference in consumption between men and women appears greater, 41% of men who smoked compared with 30% of women smoking 20 cigarettes or more a day. Again, the gap widens with age, nearly 60% of men compared with 40% of women aged 45-54. (Figure 2.11)

Consumption measured according to taryield also portrays lower figures for women than men. In 1994 women smokers were more likely than men smokers to smoke filter cigarettes, 96% compared with 78%, the difference being largely due to the higher percentage of men who smoked hand-rolled cigarettes.[7] The difference between men and women smokers in type of cigarette smoked narrows among younger age groups, there being 90% of men smokers aged 16-19 and 96% of women smokers aged 16-19 who smoked filter cigarettes. Women were more likely than men to smoke low tar cigarettes, 37% compared with 24% of those who smoked manufactured cigarettes in 1994, or 36% compared with 19% of all cigarette smokers. (Figure 2.12)

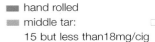

low to middle tar:
10 but less than 15mg/cig

hand rolled

middle tar:
15 but less than18mg/cig

low tar:
less than 10mg/cig

Figure 2.12	Tar level and type of cigarette smoked by sex: Great Britain 1994

Source: General Household Survey

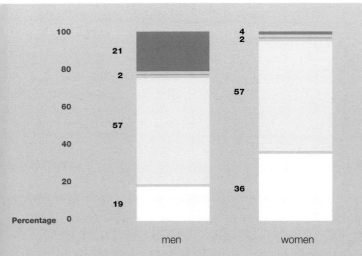

National and regional differences in cigarette smoking

Cigarette smoking varies with place of residence in the UK; 27% in England and Northern Ireland, 28% in Wales and 30% in Scotland.[8] (Figure 2.13) Regional gradients within England compare with those at national level: higher in Greater London and the Northern regions, 28-29%, than in the Central and Southern regions, 24-26%.

Social class differentials in cigarette smoking

There are large social class differentials in cigarette smoking which persist among men and women and irrespective of age (Figure 2.14). A lower proportion of men and women in social classes I-II (professional, managerial and technical occupations) smoke cigarettes or have ever smoked cigarettes than those in social classes IV-V (partly skilled and unskilled occupations). A consistent social class gradient in smoking characterises the figures for men of all ages and women under 65. Higher smoking levels among those under 25 in social classes I-II than in social class IIIN (skilled non-manual occupations) may be real, but equally may be due to social class in this age group being more fluid and less well-defined.

Figure 2.13 Percentage who smoke cigarettes by country and region: UK 1994

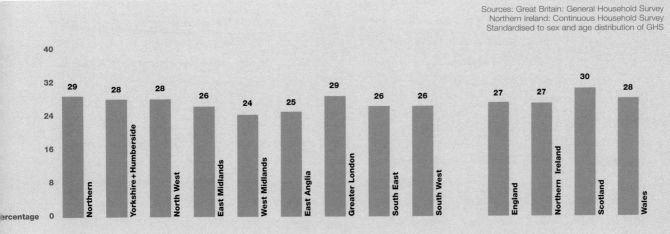

Sources: Great Britain: General Household Survey
Northern Ireland: Continuous Household Survey
Standardised to sex and age distribution of GHS

Figure 2.14 Percentage current and ex-cigarette smokers by social class, sex and age: Great Britain 1994

Social class
order within age I-II IIIN IIIM IV-V

■ current smokers
□ ex-smokers

Source: General Household Survey

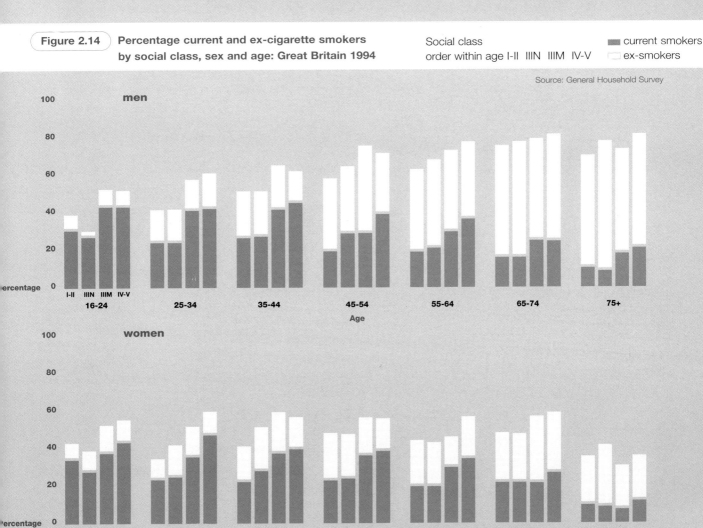

TRENDS IN CIGARETTE SMOKING

Trends in the prevalence of cigarette smoking

Present smoking status by age reflects individual lifetime effects in terms of starting and quitting as well as earlier cigarette smoking levels overall, associated with fashion and awareness of its harmful effects. To appreciate ongoing and likely future consequences for mortality in the UK requires knowledge of trends in cigarette smoking.

Direct estimates of the proportions of adults who smoke cigarettes are available for the period 1948 to the present[9] (Figure 3.1). Cigarette smoking among men has been falling gradually since the late 1940s, though most steadily and steeply during the 1970s and 1980s. In 1948 nearly two in three men aged 16 or more smoked cigarettes. By the early 1970s the figure had fallen to just over one in two and by 1994 to 28%. The most recent figure, 29% in 1996, marks for the first time since the 1970s a halt in the downward trend. A lower proportion of women than men smoked cigarettes in 1948, but prevalence increased gradually, peaking around 44% in the late 1960s. Prevalence for women started falling steadily thereafter, less steeply than among men, to 26% in 1994. Just as for men the 1996 figure, 28%, suggests a slight upturn in cigarette smoking. It is impossible to gauge however whether this is spurious or signifies a genuine increase.

The steady fall in prevalence during the 1970s and 1980s reflects recognition and greater awareness of the mortality and morbidity consequences of smoking and the emphasis, especially among men, on reducing prevalence. A later and gentler decline in cigarette smoking among women than men means a gradual convergence between the two.

The figures by age depict a levelling off in prevalence at younger ages. Cigarette smoking among men and women aged 16-24 years fell gradually until the early-to-mid 1980s, since when it has remained more or less the same, with a slight increase in the 1990s (Figure 3.2, Annex A, Table A1). Slightly higher levels among men aged 16-24 than women in the past had disappeared also by the mid-1980s.

The figures suggest a similar though more recent levelling off and slight increase among those aged 25-34 and a levelling off among those aged 35-44 years. (Figure 3.3a: men, Figure 3.3b: women)

Between 1994 and 1996 a levelling off or more commonly a slight increase in cigarette smoking was recorded in all age groups of men and women.

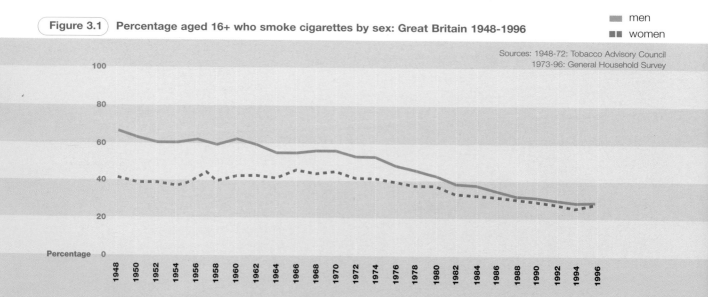

Figure 3.1 **Percentage aged 16+ who smoke cigarettes by sex: Great Britain 1948-1996**

legend: men, women

Sources: 1948-72: Tobacco Advisory Council
1973-96: General Household Survey

3

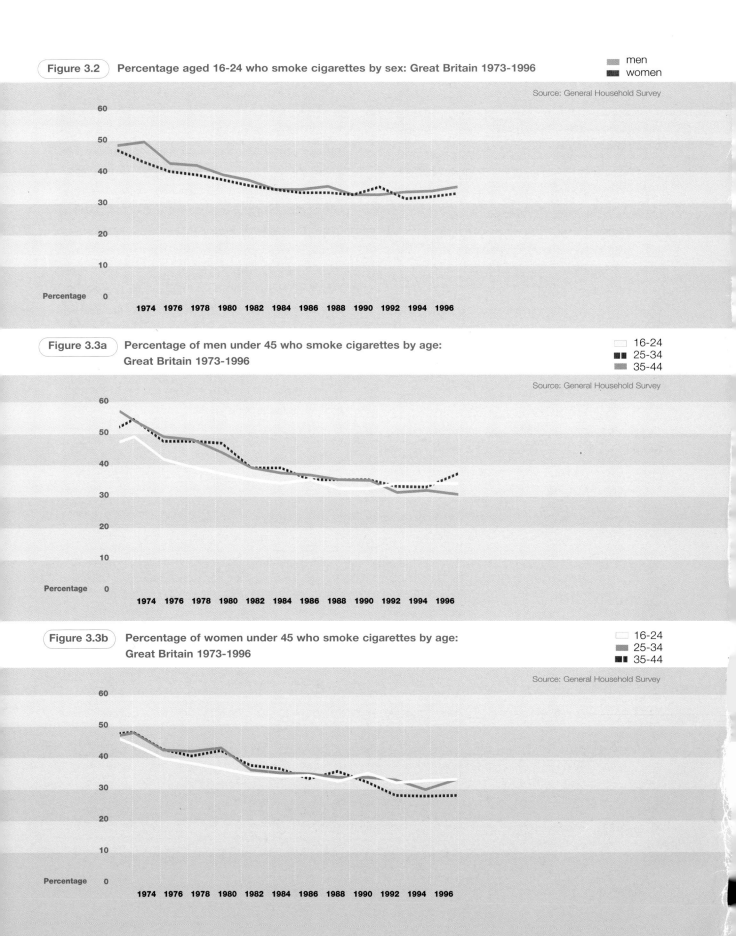

Figure 3.2   Percentage aged 16-24 who smoke cigarettes by sex: Great Britain 1973-1996

men
women

Source: General Household Survey

Figure 3.3a   Percentage of men under 45 who smoke cigarettes by age:
Great Britain 1973-1996

16-24
25-34
35-44

Source: General Household Survey

Figure 3.3b   Percentage of women under 45 who smoke cigarettes by age:
Great Britain 1973-1996

16-24
25-34
35-44

Source: General Household Survey

The trends in smoking among those aged 11-15 years project further increases in prevalence among young adults (Figure 3.4). Cigarette smoking in this age group initially seems to have peaked in 1984, falling until 1988 before rising again in the 1990s to reach levels in 1996 which for boys were just below and for girls exceeded the earlier peak. Ever since 1986 girls aged 11-15 have been more likely than boys to smoke cigarettes.

Trends in cigarette smoking among young people chiefly reflect trends in the likelihood of their starting to smoke. Thus the trends by age in the percentage who have ever been cigarette smokers also portray a stabilising at younger ages. (Annex A, Table A2)

Cigarette smoking rates at older ages are increasingly influenced by trends in quitting rates. Quitting rates among men aged under 45 appear to have changed little or have fallen between the 1980s and 1994. (Figure 3.5, Annex A, Table A3)

Though rising until 1994, quitting rates for women over 45 have throughout been lower than those for men. The 1996 figures register a levelling off or reduction in quitting rates in almost all age groups of men and women. Lower quitting rates recorded in 1996 than in 1994 appear to account for much of the apparent increase in levels of cigarette smoking, lending some support to this being a genuine period effect.

Overall the figures for the mid-1990s provide evidence of a slowing down or arrest in the decline in cigarette smoking, measured by the proportion who start cigarette smoking or the proportion of cigarette smokers who quit smoking. The most recent figures moreover suggest a slight increase in both respects in cigarette smoking but it is as yet too soon to assess how real this is.

3

Figure 3.4 Percentage aged 11-15 years who smoke cigarettes by sex: England 1982-1996

■ boys
□ girls

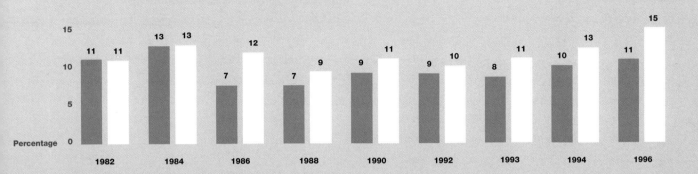

Source: *Smoking among secondary school children*

Figure 3.5 Percentage of ever smokers who have quit smoking
by sex and age, 1973-1996: Great Britain

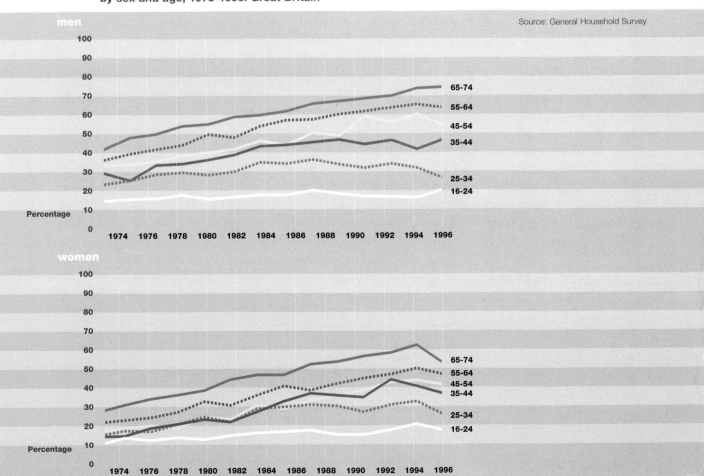

Source: General Household Survey

Trends in social class differentials in cigarette smoking

A key feature of the recent history of the UK smoking epidemic is the large social class differential. In 1973, nearly 60% of men in manual classes were smokers compared with about 45% in the non-manual groups, the figures falling respectively to 34% and 22% in 1994 (Figure 3.6). About 45% of women in manual classes were smokers in 1973, and just under 40% of those in non-manual classes, falling to 31% and 21% respectively by 1994. The widening of the gap between the early 1970s and mid-to-late 1980s is in part the latter stages of the emergence of social class differentials from the earlier undifferentiated epidemic. It may be due in part also to an earlier decline among the non-manual than manual groups, as a slight narrowing in the 1990s suggests. It is however difficult to gauge detailed underlying trends on the basis of this crude breakdown, and finer breakdowns by other measures of social and economic situation may be more illuminating and relevant.

The more gradual reduction in cigarette smoking among women than men was replicated within social class, and within class convergence between the two the result. Thus as sex differentials in smoking within social class practically disappeared, social class has become a key differentiating factor in smoking behaviour.

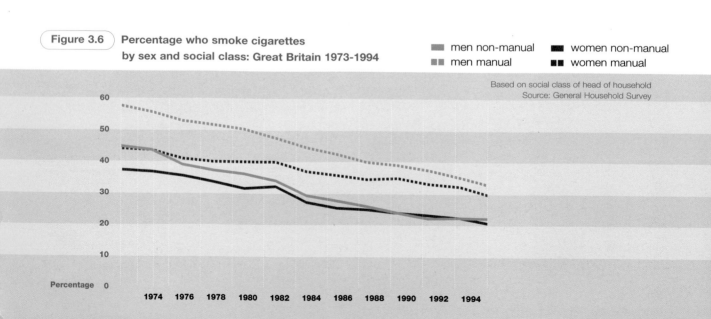

Figure 3.6 **Percentage who smoke cigarettes by sex and social class: Great Britain 1973-1994**

men non-manual   women non-manual
men manual   women manual

Based on social class of head of household
Source: General Household Survey

Percentage

Trends in consumption

In the late 1970s and early 1980s about 50% of men who smoked cigarettes were heavy smokers, smoking 20 cigarettes or more a day (Figure 3.7). The figure fell, to around 45% in the period 1984 to 1990, falling again in the 1990s, to 38% in 1996. There has been relatively little change among women in the proportion who smoke 20 or more cigarettes a day. Around 36% of women who smoked in the late 1970s and early 1980s were heavy smokers, falling to 32% in 1984 and 30% in 1996.

There was a small increase between 1974 and 1990 in the proportion who smoked filter cigarettes, figures remaining fairly stable during the 1990s. (Figure 3.8)

Since the mid-1980s there has been a notable increase, especially between 1992 and 1994, in the proportion who smoked low-tar cigarettes. (Figure 3.9)

Measured in terms of number or type of cigarette smoked, cigarette consumption throughout the period was lower among women than men.

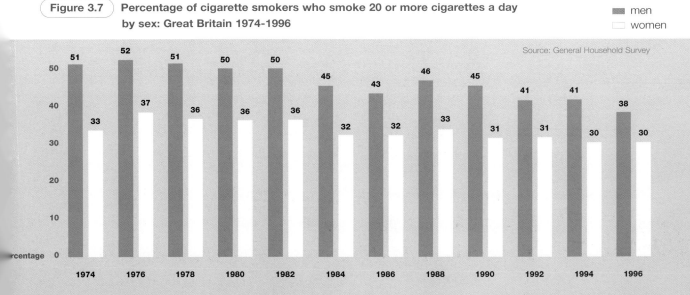

Figure 3.7 **Percentage of cigarette smokers who smoke 20 or more cigarettes a day by sex: Great Britain 1974-1996**

■ men
□ women

Source: General Household Survey

Figure 3.8 Percentage of cigarette smokers who smoke filter cigarettes by sex: Great Britain 1974-1994

■ men
☐ women

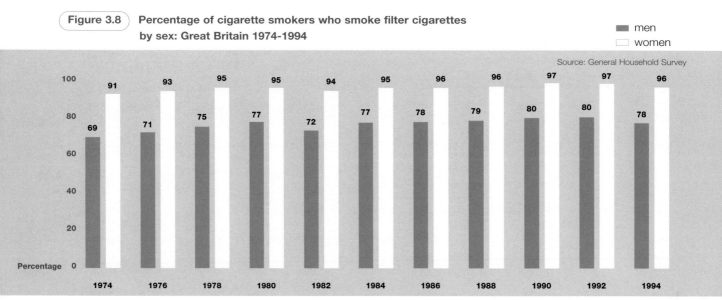

Source: General Household Survey

Percentage

Figure 3.9 Percentage smoking low-tar cigarettes of those who smoke manufactured cigarettes by sex: Great Britain 1986-1994

■ men
☐ women

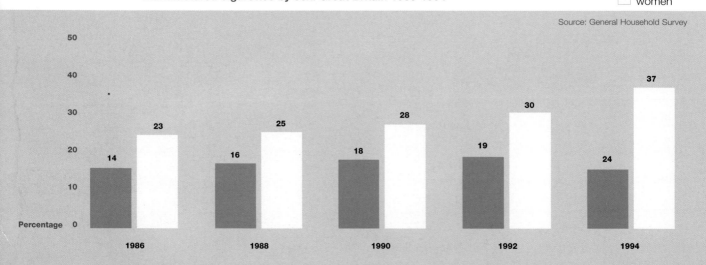

Source: General Household Survey

Percentage

TRENDS IN **CIGARETTE** **SMOKING** AND **MORTALITY**

Trends in cigarette smoking during the twentieth century

To assess properly ongoing trends in mortality outcomes, it is necessary to look further back to trends in cigarette smoking in the first half of the twentieth century; people aged 70 years or more in 1995 for example were born in or before 1925, and would probably have started smoking prior to 1950. This period was the hey-day for the cigarette, before people were aware of the fatal consequences.

Figures for cigarette smoking prevalence prior to 1948 are not directly available. Cigarette smoking earlier in the century can however be gleaned from the percentages in the past who ever became cigarette smokers[10] (Figure 4.1). This is the period before the harmful effects of smoking cigarettes were commonly known, and before quitting smoking in response to it became a significant feature in smoking behaviour. During this time therefore, ever-smoking provides a reasonable proxy for current cigarette smoking. Assuming that they started smoking at age 16 years on average, the figures of ever-smoking for cohorts depict an impression of cigarette smoking at the time that they would have started smoking.

That cigarette smoking was ubiquitous in the past among men in Great Britain is undeniable. More than four in five men born in the period 1900-1929, who would have been

aged 16 in 1916-1945, became cigarette smokers. Acquiring the smoking habit became less common among those born later, falling to around one in two of those born after 1960. For women the picture is quite different; one in three of those born in the period 1900-1904 became cigarette smokers, rising to a peak of around three in five of those born in the decade 1920-1929, who would have started smoking around world war two. The figures depict a slight decline among those born in the 1930s, who would have started smoking in the post-second world war period, rising very slightly among those aged 16 in 1956-1965, falling gradually again for those aged 16 in 1966-1980. The most recent figures, for those born in 1965-69, who would have been aged 16 in 1981-1986, suggest a slight increase in ever-smoking. This is consistent with rising smoking levels among 11-15 year olds in the early 1980s, the 1965-69 cohort aged 11-15 years in 1980.

The figures demonstrate the later timing and lower peak of the smoking epidemic in the UK for women than men. They illustrate the gradual closing of the gap in cigarette smoking between men and women, with figures for the most recent cohort suggesting a reversing of the differential.

Figure 4.1 Percentage who ever smoked cigarettes by sex and year of birth: Great Britain

■■ men
■■ women

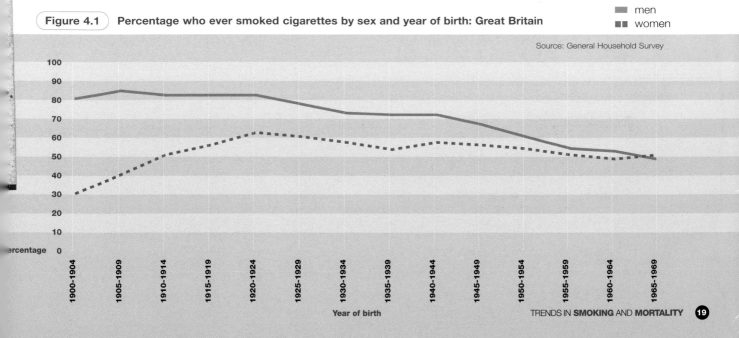

Source: General Household Survey

Year of birth

4

Trends in mortality outcomes of smoking

Cigarette smoking is the predominant risk factor for lung cancer, accounting for the majority of deaths from the disease. Trends in lung cancer death rates therefore can be used to illustrate the mortality impact of the UK smoking epidemic.

The trends by age over the last forty years portray lung cancer death rates rising and then falling, the timing of the peak varying with age group[11](Table 4.1). In the case of men for example, lung cancer death rates in the age group 65-69 were highest in 1966-70, in the age group 70-74 five years later in 1971-75, age 75-79 in 1976-80 and age 80-84 in 1981-85. The figures depict a cohort of men who experienced higher lung cancer mortality than those born before or after, visible in their death rates at each age. Analysis of age-specific mortality rates by period of birth has identified men born around the turn of the century as the cohorts with the highest lung cancer mortality rates throughout their adult life.[12]

The figures for women are much more definitive, highest 40-44 year lung cancer mortality in 1966-1970, 45-49 years in 1971-1975 and five years later for each subsequent age group. Rates at age 60-64 peaked in 1986-1990, indicating lung cancer mortality rates for the age group 65-69 peaked in 1991-1995 and in the age group 70-74 projected to peak in 1996-2000. The cohort who experienced the highest mortality rates have been identified as women born around 1926.

Comparison of trends in cigarette smoking and lung cancer death rates provides evidence of the direct link between smoking and lung cancer. The cohort of men born around 1900 who experienced the highest lung cancer death rates at each age are also the ones among whom cigarette smoking reached its peak. The picture is clearer for women, among whom the smoking epidemic occurred more recently, with highest death rates occurring for women born in the mid-1920s, the cohort among whom cigarette smoking reached its peak.

By 1995, the year for which numbers of deaths caused by smoking are estimated in this report, lung cancer mortality rates for men had passed the peak and were falling among all age groups. Lung cancer death rates for women aged 65-69 had reached their peak and for the age group 70 and over were yet to do so. The rates were falling at younger ages and still increasing at older ages as those born in the 1920s reached the highest ages of mortality.

4

Table 4.1 Lung cancer death rates by sex and age 1951–1995: Great Britain

Deaths per 100,000

	1951-55	1956-60	1961-65	1966-70	1971-75	1976-80	1981-85	1986-90	1991-95
men									
35-39	10.2	9.5	9.5	7.7	5.9	5.4	4.2	3.4	2.7
40-44	25.1	25.6	22.9	22.5	18.0	13.9	12.0	10.4	8.5
45-49	59.1	59.9	57.5	54.0	51.0	40.1	32.2	27.6	22.5
50-54	124.4	126.2	124.1	117.0	108.1	100.9	78.0	60.0	54.8
55-59	202.4	232.6	231.9	222.6	209.0	190.8	173.1	135.0	105.9
60-64	256.4	336.8	371.6	371.9	355.4	334.6	302.1	269.1	201.5
65-69	290.9	394.4	488.2	530.4	519.5	497.7	457.4	412.9	357.3
70-74	256.8	386.1	497.4	621.3	682.5	669.2	633.6	585.0	497.0
75-79	202.6	328.9	449.4	593.3	724.3	798.7	775.3	713.5	619.2
80-84	141.3	222.1	336.7	452.5	605.8	763.8	839.5	797.5	706.9
women									
35-39	2.8	3.1	3.2	3.1	2.8	2.7	2.5	2.1	1.8
40-44	5.2	6.3	7.1	8.2	7.0	6.5	6.1	6.3	6.2
45-49	8.9	10.5	14.0	16.4	18.7	16.4	14.7	14.1	13.9
50-54	13.9	17.1	21.9	28.6	33.9	37.4	31.5	27.6	28.0
55-59	20.7	24.3	30.8	40.1	50.4	58.3	65.0	58 3	46.7
60-64	28.6	33.1	42.4	51.2	67.8	86.9	99.2	113.1	93.2
65-69	35.2	38.7	51.8	65.3	80.7	103.3	131.3	149.6	153.7
70-74	39.1	45.4	54.8	72.9	88.0	111.2	145.0	175.7	192.1
75-79	44.0	49.6	58.0	74.0	90.1	113.4	146.2	179.6	198.8
80-84	39.8	45.9	56.4	67.1	86.8	106.0	136.0	166.3	187.2

Shaded death rates are maximum for age group

Tar yield and mortality

'Tar' measured as total particulate matter less moisture and nicotine is an index of the carcinogenic potential of cigarette smoke. Starting in the 1960s, as tobacco manufacturers responded to public acceptance of the message that smoking kills, tar yield per cigarette has fallen considerably. The switch to filter cigarettes caused tar yield per cigarette to fall to 26 mg in the early 1960s, compared with 33 mg in the late 1930s.[11] By 1993, following reductions in tar yields in existing brands and the introduction of low tar brands in the late 1970s and early 1980s, average tar yield had fallen to 11 mg.

Reduction in tar yield entails also a reduction in yield of the addictive substance nicotine. Smokers, especially those addicted, tend to adapt their smoking behaviour to offset the reduction in nicotine associated with lower tar yield. Longer and more frequent puffs, shorter butts, inhaling more deeply are responses which, as well as restoring nicotine intake, increased tar exposure too. The reduction in average tar yield per cigarette, mediated through individual changes in smoking behaviour, was not translated therefore into an equivalent reduction in tar exposure. Whilst there is ample evidence of nicotine compensation in response to reduction in tar yield however, it has not yet been established whether this is 100 per cent and to what extent it is maintained in the longer term.

There is evidence that reduction in tar yield may reduce the risk of lung cancer, but no direct evidence of a beneficial effect in respect of other diseases that smoking can cause. Reductions in tar yield since the 1960s are believed to partially account for reductions in lung cancer death rates among men and women since the 1960s and to have moderated increasing death rates for age groups in which death rates had not yet peaked. For other diseases caused by smoking reduction in tar yield has no impact, changes in mortality corresponding to changes in the proportion of cigarette smokers.

Quitting smoking and mortality

Smokers who quit, even at older ages, radically lessen their mortality risks, the timing and extent of risk reduction varying with disease.

Ten years after quitting, the lung cancer risk falls to 30-50% of the risk in continuing smokers, and continues to decline thereafter.[13] Ischaemic heart disease is associated with an initial rapid reduction in risk on quitting, followed by a more gradual decline. Within a year, the excess risk falls to half or even less than that associated with continuing to smoke and after 15 years is similar to that of people who have never smoked cigarettes.

Cigarette smoking accelerates age-related decline in lung function and quitting returns the rate of decline to that in people who have never smoked cigarettes. Excess mortality risks for chronic obstructive lung disease start to fall in comparison with continuing smokers a few years after quitting. Excess mortality risks decline with years since quitting but even after 20 years or more the risk of chronic obstructive lung disease mortality remains higher than for never smokers.

Overall it has been shown, based on the risks of dying from all diseases according to the time since quitting, that the reduction in risk for smokers begins shortly after giving up smoking and continues for at least 10 to 15 years. After 10-15 years, the risk of all-cause mortality returns nearly to that of persons who have never smoked.

4

Effect of ongoing trends in cigarette smoking

On the basis of trends in lung cancer death rates it is projected that death rates from smoking among women aged 70-74 will peak during the next five years, those among women aged 75-79 continuing to rise until 2001-2005 and among women aged 80-84 until 2006-2010. Death rates in younger age groups of women and in all age groups of men are expected to continue to fall as the maximum impact of the large reductions in cigarette smoking of the 1970s and 1980s is felt.

The increase in absolute numbers of deaths among women due to smoking is expected to continue over the next decade. The projected numbers of deaths depend not only on death rates however, but also on population numbers by age. The cohort of women experiencing the highest death rates from smoking were born during a period when birth rates were falling, and the expected increase in number of deaths unlikely to be as large as the projected increase in death rates might suggest. On the other hand the post-second world war 'baby boom', aged 60 after 2005, is likely to have an inflationary influence on absolute number of deaths from smoking for men and women in coming decades even though death rates from smoking are falling.

The apparent increase in smoking among younger people would, other things being equal, project increasing death rates from smoking several decades in the future: those born in 1965 reaching age 60 in 2025, and those aged 15 in 1996 age 60 in 2041.

The closing of the gap between cigarette smoking for men and women signifies a narrowing in future of the gap in death rates from smoking. Past widening social class differentials in smoking on the other hand signify an increase in social class differentials in deaths due to smoking, especially among women.

The smoking epidemic has already had such a large impact on patterns of UK mortality that it has reduced the female advantage in life expectancy.[14] Between 1971 and 1993 the advantage for women in life expectancy at age 60 years fell from 4.5 years to 4.1 years and at age 50 from 5.3 to 4.5 years. That this is due to the effects of smoking is evidenced by the fact that the female advantage in life expectancy at age 70, comprised entirely of the mortality experience of women prior to the peak of the epidemic, increased from 3.0 to 3.2 years. As equalisation in smoking rates works through into mortality it is expected that the female advantage will reduce still further.

Conversely the structural impact on mortality of social class differentials in smoking is expected to shift existing social class differentials in mortality to an even greater order of magnitude.

5

DEATHS DUE TO SMOKING IN 1995

Estimating deaths due to smoking

Cigarette smoking kills people as a result of the diseases it causes. These range across the spectrum, including cancer, circulatory disease, respiratory and digestive disease. Smokers have higher death rates from each disease than people who have never smoked and, with much higher death rates overall than never smokers, there is a high probability that they will die prematurely from their habit. Ex-smokers' death rates are also usually higher than death rates for people who have never smoked cigarettes. Since the risks fall notably after quitting however, the excess risk is much less than for those who continue to smoke.

People who have never smoked cigarettes die from diseases which smoking can cause, though their risks of doing so are less than that of smokers. Smokers start with the same mortality risks as never-smokers, but they significantly increase their risks by smoking cigarettes. Smokers can die therefore from a disease which smoking can cause but not on account of their smoking.

The proportion of deaths associated with smoking varies both with the extent to which smoking can cause the disease and with the importance of other causes. It is high in the case of lung cancer for example, for which smoking is the main cause. For ischaemic heart disease on the other hand smoking is one of several causes, such as a high saturated fat diet and high blood pressure. The proportion associated with smoking is accordingly lower. A larger number of possible causes however may be expected to cause more deaths overall, so that a lower proportion may nevertheless result in more absolute numbers of deaths caused by smoking.

Deaths from smoking cannot be estimated directly. Individuals who die from their smoking cannot be identified. Even were smoking status included on the death certificate it would not be possible to identify which deaths were actually caused by smoking since a proportion of smokers, albeit small for some diseases, die from a disease that smoking can cause, not on account of their smoking but due to other causes of the disease.

Deaths from smoking are estimated by comparing death rates for current smokers and ex-smokers with death rates for never smokers. The extent to which smoking adds to the mortality risks of never smokers can be used to estimate the number or proportion of deaths caused by smoking. This cannot be done directly from national statistics since without knowing smoking status of the deceased, death rates of current smokers, ex-smokers and never smokers cannot be calculated. Were never smokers' death rates transferable across place and time it would still be possible to estimate deaths due to smoking by subtraction from the death rate in the population. This can only be justified in the case of lung cancer, however and instead indirect methods are used based on relative risks.

To estimate the number of UK deaths caused by smoking in 1995, an approach similar to that used for the previous HEA estimate was used.[1] It is in essence the same as that applied by the United States Surgeon-General to estimate deaths in the US caused by smoking.[15] The excess risks of ex-smokers as well as current smokers are taken into account. The proportion of deaths from each disease due to smoking is derived from the proportions who are smokers and ex-smokers, and an estimate of their excess mortality risk – their risk of dying from the disease relative to that of people who have never been smokers.

The diseases included in the present estimate are listed, with revisions since the previous estimate indicated, in Table 5.1. (Annex B)

Table 5.1 Diseases included in the estimate of death by smoking

Diseases caused by smoking	ICD Code-9th Revision
Cancer	
Lung	162
Upper respiratory sites	140-149, 161
Oesophagus	150
Bladder	188
Kidney	189
Stomach	151
Pancreas	157
Unspecified site*	199
Myeloid leukaemia*	205
Respiratory	
Chronic obstructive lung disease	490-492,496
Pneumonia*	480-487
Circulatory	
Ischaemic heart disease	410-414
Cerebrovascular disease	430-438
Aortic aneurysm	441
Myocardial degeneration*	429
Atherosclerosis*	440
Digestive	
Ulcer of stomach + duodenum	531-533
Diseases prevented by smoking	
Parkinson's disease*	332
Endometrial cancer*	182

Diseases added since previous estimate indicated by *
Cancer of the cervix no longer included (see Annex B)

5

Estimates of relative mortality for each disease were derived from the American Cancer Society's prospective study in the 1980s of one million adults in the US, which represents the best available approximation to the UK. (Annex C for selection and Annex D for estimation). This study was not representative of the US as a whole, over-representing the more highly educated and under-representing the most disadvantaged, but though absolute mortality rates were lower than those of the general population this should not invalidate relative risks. Cigarette smokers and ex-smokers in the study population and the UK were found furthermore to be sufficiently alike in respect of past exposure to cigarette smoke to justify application of relative risks from the study to the UK.

Based on relative mortality risks for each disease, together with percentages of current and ex-smokers by age, the percentages by age of deaths from each disease due to smoking were derived for men and women separately. (Annex E)

Deaths from lung cancer were estimated using this approach and a second set of estimates also produced based, as described earlier, on the difference between UK death rates and never smokers' lung cancer death rates. The method assumes equivalence between UK and American Cancer Society never-smokers' lung cancer mortality and deaths caused by smoking are estimated by subtracting American Cancer Society never smokers' age-specific lung cancer mortality rates from UK age-specific lung cancer mortality rates.[16] Both sets of estimates are presented, though to maintain consistency with the approach to other diseases the former is used in the analysis that follows.

Number of deaths by disease due to smoking

In 1995 an estimated 121,700 people died from smoking in the UK. This amounts on average to 2,300 deaths every week, 330 every day and 14 deaths every hour caused by smoking.

80,400 men and 41,300 women were estimated to have died from cigarette smoking in UK in 1995; every day 220 men and 110 women and every hour 9 men and 5 women died on average as a result of their smoking.

Nine in ten deaths from lung cancer among men are estimated to have been caused by smoking, and nearly three in four (73%) among women - 84% of all lung cancer deaths. (Table 5.2) The estimates are even higher, especially for women, when based on the difference between UK death rates and American Cancer Society study never smokers' death rates; 92% of lung cancer deaths among men, more than four in five (82%) of those among women and nearly nine in ten (89%) of all lung cancer deaths caused by smoking.

Nearly nine in ten deaths (86%) from chronic obstructive lung disease for men and four in five (79%) for women were caused by smoking.

Nearly one in four deaths from ischaemic heart disease among men were caused by smoking, and one in ten among women, 17% in all. Cigarette smoking accounts for a much higher percentage of deaths from ischaemic heart disease and stroke at younger ages, and there is little difference in the figures for men and women. More than two in five (45%) deaths from ischaemic heart disease among men aged under 65 years and 40% among women, 44% in all, were caused by smoking. Likewise two in five deaths under 65 from stroke are estimated to have been caused by smoking.

Table 5.2 Number and percentage of deaths estimated to be caused by smoking by disease: UK 1995

	Number of deaths from disease estimated to be caused by smoking			Percentage of all deaths from disease estimated to be caused by smoking		
	men	women	total	men	women	total
Diseases caused in part by smoking						
Cancer						
Lung	21,100	9,500	30,600	90	73	84
Lung [1]	21,700	10,700	32,400	92	82	89
Upper respiratory sites	1,500	400	1,900	74	47	66
Oesophagus	2,900	1,600	4,500	71	62	67
Bladder	1,700	300	2,000	48	17	38
Kidney	700	100	800	41	5	27
Stomach	1,700	300	2,000	35	10	25
Pancreas	600	800	1,500	21	25	23
Unspecified site	2,400	500	3,000	34	7	20
Unspecified site [2]	4,100	1,300	5,400	57	17	51
Myeloid leukaemia	200	100	300	19	10	15
Respiratory						
Chronic obstructive lung disease	15,100	9,300	24,400	86	79	83
Pneumonia	5,800	4,100	9,900	25	11	16
Circulatory						
Ischaemic heart disease	18,700	7,600	26,400	23	11	17
35-64	7,500	1,900	9,400	45	40	44
65+	11,200	5,800	17,000	17	9	13
Cerebrovascular disease	3,400	3,900	7,300	13	9	11
35-64	1,100	900	2,100	40	41	41
65+	2,200	3,000	5,200	10	7	8
Aortic aneurysm	4,000	1,800	5,800	62	48	57
Myocardial degeneration	300	300	600	24	10	15
Atherosclerosis	100	100	200	17	5	9
Digestive						
Ulcer of stomach + duodenum	1,000	1,000	1,900	47	41	44
Total caused by smoking	81,300	41,700	123,000			
Diseases prevented in part by smoking						
Parkinson's	900	300	1,200	57	24	42
Endometrial cancer	N/A	100	100	N/A	15	15
Total prevented by smoking	900	400	1,300			
Deaths from all causes due to smoking						
(caused less prevented)	80,400	41,300	121,700			

[1] Subtracting American Cancer Society never-smokers' death rates from UK death rates, see text, p. 26

[2] Based on all deaths from cancer of unspecified site-see Annex B

N/A: not applicable

Number of deaths rounded to nearest 00, so totals may not add up

Percentages based on unrounded figures

5

Considered by disease group the impact of cigarette smoking is equally significant (Figure 5.1, Table 5.3). It is estimated to have caused two in five of all deaths from cancer among men and nearly one in five among women, 30% of all deaths from cancer in 1995. Considering all deaths from respiratory disease, cigarette smoking was responsible for 45% in the case of men and one in four in the case of women, one in three of all such deaths. In the group of diseases of the digestive system it is estimated to have been the cause of one in ten deaths.

When all deaths from diseases of the circulatory system are considered, cigarette smoking is estimated to account for one in five among men and nearly one in ten among women, 15% of all deaths. Many such deaths occur in older age groups, when other causes become more prominent relative to cigarette smoking than at younger ages. Considering only deaths under 65 years it is estimated that cigarette smoking caused nearly two in five deaths among men and 31% among women, more than one in three (36%) in all.

Differences in the percentage of deaths caused by smoking to a large extent reflect the significance of other causes of the disease. The mortality impact by disease, and the scope for prevention, can better be assessed by comparing total numbers of deaths. (Figure 5.2)

In these terms, lung cancer, ischaemic heart disease and chronic obstructive lung disease are closer than implied by the percentages caused by smoking; 30,600 deaths from lung cancer, 24,400 from chronic obstructive lung disease and 26,400 from ischaemic heart disease.

The figures by disease group demonstrate the across-the-board impact of cigarette smoking: 46,000 deaths from cancer, 34,000 from respiratory diseases, 40,000 from circulatory diseases and 2,000 from digestive diseases.

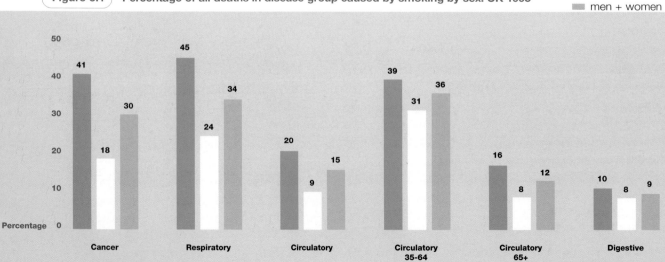

Figure 5.1   **Percentage of all deaths in disease group caused by smoking by sex: UK 1995**

men
women
men + women

Table 5.3 Deaths caused by disease group: UK 1995

Disease group	Number of deaths			Percentage of all deaths caused by smoking		
	men	women	total	men	women	total
Cancer	32,800	13,700	46,500	41	18	30
(140-208)						
Respiratory disease	20,900	13,400	34,300	45	24	34
(390-519)						
Circulatory disease	26,600	13,700	40,300	20	9	15
(390-459)						
35-64	9,200	2,900	12,100	39	31	36
65+	17,400	10,800	28,200	16	8	12
Digestive disease	1,000	1,000	1,900	10	8	9
(520-579)						

Figures in parentheses ICD-9 codes
Numbers of deaths rounded to nearest 00
Percentages based on unrounded figures

There is evidence that smoking reduces the risk of a few diseases and this needs to be weighed against the substantial harm. With respect to Parkinson's disease and endometrial cancer smoking exerts a protective effect which appears to relate to nicotine and an estimated 1,300 deaths from these diseases were prevented by smoking. This compares however with 123,000 caused by smoking, nearly one hundred times as many deaths due to smoking as prevented by smoking. The health benefits of active smoking therefore are negligible and are far outweighed by the substantial risks.

Figure 5.2 Deaths caused by smoking by disease

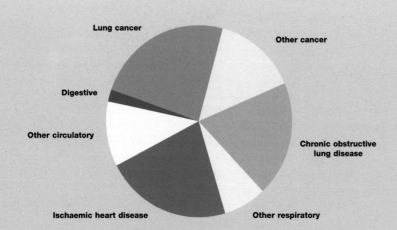

Cigarette smoking in relation to all deaths

Cigarette smoking caused 121,700 out of a total of 644,000 UK deaths at all ages in 1995 (Figure 5.3).[17] Nearly one in five (19%) deaths in 1995 therefore were due to smoking. For men this represented more than one in four deaths and for women nearly one in eight.

The figures for deaths under 65 are even more striking. More than one in four (28%) deaths of people aged 35-64 are estimated to have been caused by their smoking, one in three deaths among men and one in five deaths among women (Figure 5.4, Table 5.4). The figures for deaths under age 65 are more alike for men and women than at older ages, the effect of a convergence in cigarette smoking at younger ages.

Cigarette smoking elevated the UK death rate in 1995 by 23% (Figure 5.5). Deaths under 65 years were nearly 40% higher than they would have been in the absence of smoking, and in the case of men under 65, cigarette smoking is estimated to have elevated the death rate by 50%.

Likewise in respect of groups of diseases, cigarette smoking caused deaths from cancer to be elevated by more than 40% and from respiratory disease by 50%. (Figure 5.6) For men, deaths from cancer were elevated by nearly 70% and from respiratory disease by 80% on account of cigarette smoking. Deaths of men and women under 65 from circulatory disease are estimated to be nearly 60% higher than they would have been in the absence of smoking.

Figure 5.3   **Deaths due to smoking as a percentage of all deaths: UK 1995**

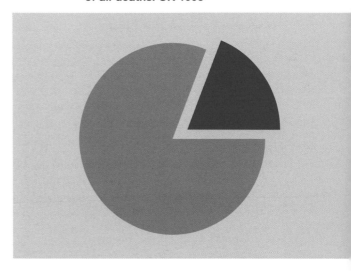

Figure 5.4   **Deaths due to smoking as a percentage of all deaths by sex and age: UK 1995**

■ men
☐ women
▨ men + women

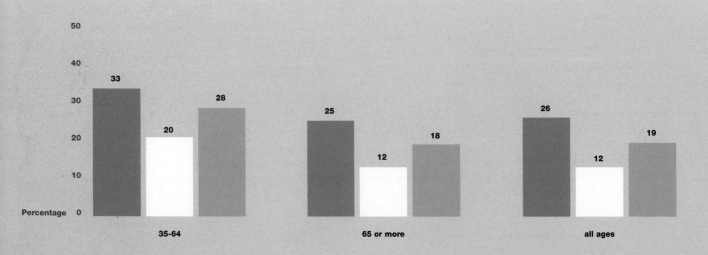

Table 5.4 Deaths under and over 65 caused by smoking: UK 1995

Age group	Number of deaths			Percentage of all deaths caused by smoking		
	men	women	total	men	women	total
35-64	19,200	7,400	26,700	33	20	28
65 or more	61,200	33,800	95,000	25	12	18
All ages*	80,400	41,300	121,700	26	12	19

* Deaths age 35 or more, percentage of deaths at all ages
Number of deaths rounded to nearest 00
Percentage based on unrounded figures

Figure 5.5 Percentage excess deaths due to smoking: UK 1995

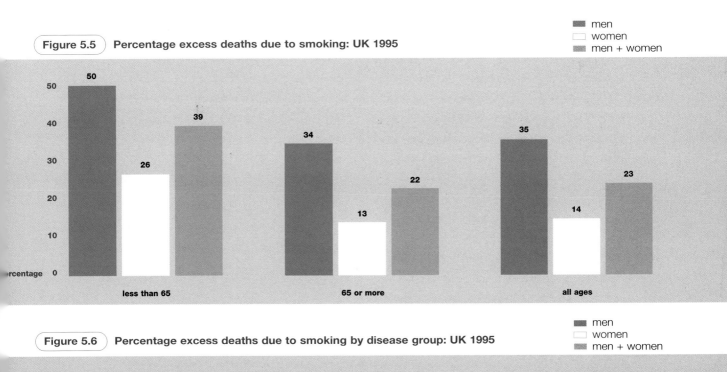

Figure 5.6 Percentage excess deaths due to smoking by disease group: UK 1995

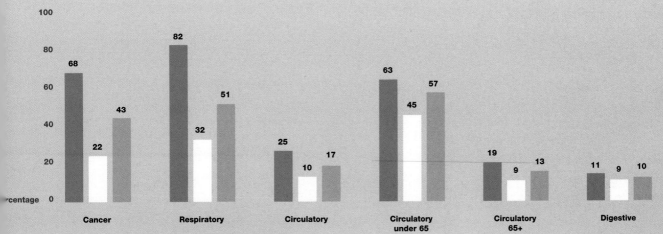

'Lifetime' effects of smoking

Another way of assessing the overall mortality impact of smoking is to look at 'lifetime' effects - how much 'sooner' will a smoker die because of their smoking, or how much smoking shortens a smoker's life. This can be assessed by constructing life tables, which summarise the experience of current smokers, ex-smokers and never smokers if they were exposed throughout their life to the prevailing mortality rates. (Annex F)

A 35 year old man who smokes cigarettes can expect to die more than seven years earlier on average than a man who has never smoked (Figure 5.7). Even for those who survive to age 65, cigarette smoking curtails expected life-span by more than six years. Expected life at age 65 years for never smokers is 1.7 times that of cigarette smokers. The figures for ex-smokers lie between the two, slightly closer to never than current smokers. At age 35 years an ex-smoker can expect to live four years longer and at age 65 more than three years longer than a man who continues to smoke cigarettes.

Cigarette smoking shortens life expectancy at age 35 years for women by six years when compared with a woman who has never smoked cigarettes (Figure 5.8). Women smokers who survive to age 65 years will die more than five years earlier on average than those who have never smoked. Never smokers' expected life at age 65 years is 1.4 times

that of current smokers. Ex-smokers have improved survival chances when compared with current smokers, the advantage apparently greater than it was for men. At age 35, women who continue to smoke can expect to die more than four years earlier on average than those who have quit smoking, and at age 65 continued smoking is associated with nearly four years' loss of life compared with those who have quit smoking.

One in four men aged 35 who smoke cigarettes can expect to die before age 65 if they continue to smoke compared to one in eight of those who have never smoked (Figure 5.9). The figure for women, though not as high as for men, is still excessive, one in six of those who continue to smoke expected to die before age 65. Cigarette smokers aged 35, men or women, are twice as likely to die before they reach age 65 than those who have never smoked.

Figure 5.7 Life expectancy at age 35 and 65 years according to smoking status: men UK 1995

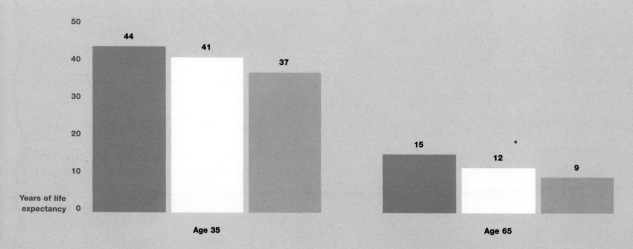

5

The likelihood of an ex-smoker aged 35 dying before age 65 years is considerably lower than for those who continue to smoke, and in the case of women just marginally higher than it is for those who have never smoked cigarettes.

Overall, an estimated one in two men (51%) who continue throughout their lives to smoke and nearly one in two women (45%) will die prematurely as a result of their smoking. For smokers who die before age 65, 56% of men and 47% of women will have been killed by their smoking.

Figure 5.8 Life expectancy at age 35 and 65 years according to smoking status: women UK 1995

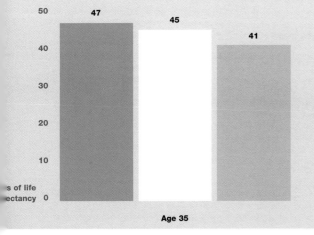

Figure 5.9 Probability of dying between age 35 and 65 by smoking status: UK 1995

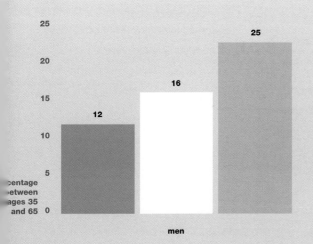
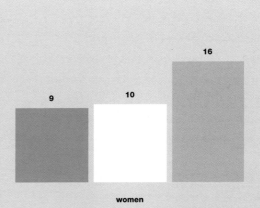

Years of life lost

The number of deaths caused by smoking does not in itself convey a sense of years of life lost to the community in the year. This depends not only on how many people died but also on the age at which they died. The latter provides an indicator of how 'premature' the deaths were compared to the age they would have died had they never smoked cigarettes. The total number of years of life lost due to deaths from smoking can be estimated from deaths from smoking by age at death and never smokers' mortality risks (Annex G).

In 1995 it is estimated that cigarette smoking caused the loss of more than 200,000 years of life under age 65 in the UK (Table 5.5). This included 150,000 years life lost for men and 60,000 for women. On average eight years under 65 were lost on account of cigarette smoking for every man or woman who died.

When the 1995 UK expectation of life instead of age 65 is used as the yardstick, the number of years of life lost on account of smoking rises to more than 600,000, that is 369,000 for men and 247,000 for women.

Table 5.5   Estimated total of years of life lost due to smoking: UK 1995

	Years of life lost before:		
	Age 65	**Age 75**	**Life expectancy***
men	152,000	400,000	369,000
women	59,000	176,000	247,000
all	211,000	576,000	616,000

* In 1995, UK life expectancy 73.9 for men and 79.2 for women
Years of life lost compared with life expectancy of a never-smoker
Figures rounded to nearest 000

National figures

The estimates presented so far are for the UK. Individual estimates were derived for constituent countries – England, Northern Ireland, Scotland and Wales. The estimates were derived using the same method as for the UK, though with national rather than UK proportions of current and ex-smokers included in the calculations. This signified small differences in percentages of deaths by disease due to smoking corresponding to national differences in cigarette smoking.

Cigarette smoking figures for Northern Ireland were derived from a different source to those for Great Britain, which may affect the apparent differentials. It may be recalled also that regional differentials in cigarette smoking within England are at least as large as those observed at national level. Differentials within England in the percentages of deaths caused by smoking will accordingly be at least as great as national differences.

The relatively small numbers of deaths by disease at national level deters production of detailed breakdowns such as provided for the UK, being subject to proportionately large yearly fluctuations and risking giving rise to an impression of spurious accuracy. Summary figures only therefore are presented.

The UK estimate of deaths caused by cigarette smoking in 1995 comprises 98,800 in England, 2,800 in Northern Ireland, 13,000 in Scotland and 7,100 deaths in Wales. (Tables 5.6, 5.7)

The percentage of all deaths caused by smoking ranges between 18% in Northern Ireland and 22% in Scotland (Figure 5.10). Similar patterns are found among men and women, ranging from 24% of all deaths for men in Northern Ireland to 28% in Scotland and for women from 12% in England and Northern Ireland to 15% in Scotland.

There is less variation in the percentage of deaths under 65 due to smoking, 28% in all except Scotland, in which an estimated 31% of deaths were caused by smoking (Figure 5.11). Deaths among those aged 65 or more range from 17% in Northern Ireland to 20% in Scotland.

Figure 5.10 Percentage of deaths due to smoking by sex and constituent countries of UK: 1995

men
women
all

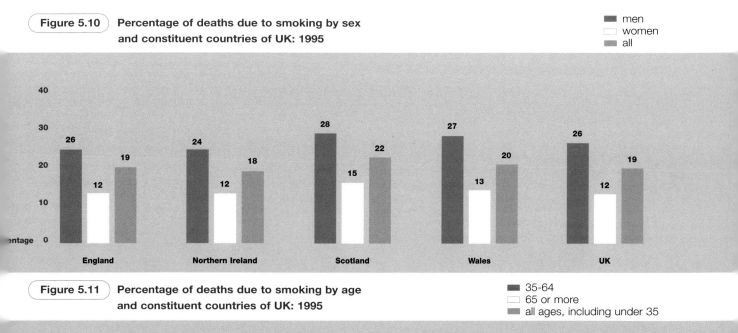

Figure 5.11 Percentage of deaths due to smoking by age and constituent countries of UK: 1995

35-64
65 or more
all ages, including under 35

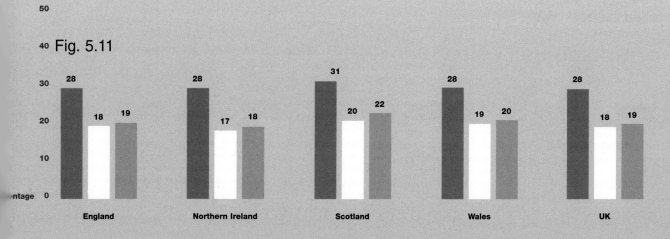

Table 5.6 National estimates of deaths due to smoking: UK 1995

Number of deaths	England	Northern Ireland	Scotland	Wales	UK
men					
Under 65	15,400	500	2,400	1,000	19,200
65+	50,400	1,300	5,800	3,600	61,200
All ages	65,800	1,800	8,100	4,600	80,400
women					
Under 65	5,800	200	1,000	500	7,400
65+	27,200	700	3,900	2,000	33,800
All ages	33,000	1,000	4,900	2,400	41,300
All					
Under 65	21,200	700	3,400	1,400	26,700
65+	77,600	2,100	9,600	5,600	95,000
All ages	98,800	2,800	13,000	7,100	121,700

Estimates rounded to nearest 00, so totals may not be consistent

Table 5.7 National estimates of deaths due to smoking by disease groups: UK 1995

Number of deaths	England	Northern Ireland	Scotland	Wales	UK
men					
Cancer	26,800	700	3,600	1,800	32,800
Lung cancer	17,200	400	2,400	1,100	21,100
Respiratory disease	17,400	500	1,700	1,300	20,900
Chronic obstructive lung disease	12,500	300	1,300	1,000	15,100
Circulatory disease	21,500	700	2,800	1,500	26,600
Ischaemic heart disease	15,100	500	2,100	1,100	18,700
Digestive disease	800	*	100	100	1,000
women					
Cancer	11,000	300	1,800	700	13,700
Lung cancer	7,600	200	1,300	500	9,500
Respiratory disease	10,800	300	1,300	800	13,400
Chronic obstructive lung disease	7,600	200	1,000	600	9,300
Circulatory disease	10,800	300	1,700	900	13,700
Ischaemic heart disease	5,900	200	1,000	500	7,600
Digestive disease	800	*	100	100	1,000
all					
Cancer	37,800	900	5,300	2,400	46,500
Lung cancer	24,800	600	3,600	1,600	30,600
Respiratory disease	28,300	800	3,000	2,100	34,300
Chronic obstructive lung disease	20,100	500	2,200	1,500	24,400
Circulatory disease	32,300	1,000	4,600	2,500	40,300
Ischaemic heart disease	21,000	700	3,100	1,600	26,400
Digestive disease	1,600	*	200	100	1,900

*less than 50   Estimates rounded to nearest 00, so totals may not be consistent

Social class

Large social class differentials in cigarette smoking were described earlier. They feature a distinct gradient in smoking for men and women. Social class differentials in smoking imply social class differentials in the percentage of deaths caused by smoking.

Social class gradients in mortality are a well-documented and long-standing feature of UK mortality, the differential widening during the 1970s and 1980s. Life expectancy at age 15 in 1986-92 was 4.2 years higher among men and 3.3 years higher among women in social classes I-II than in social classes IV-V. At age 65, life expectancy for men and women in classes I-II were respectively 2.6 and 2 years higher than in classes IV-V.[18] The latter can be compared with the estimated difference in life expectancy at age 65 between cigarette smokers and those who have never smoked cigarettes, 6.3 years for men and 5.4 for women. Smoking status differences in life expectancy at age 65 are thus more than twice as large as the difference between social classes I-II and social classes IV-V combined.

Ideally deaths due to smoking would be estimated separately by social class and then amalgamated to provide a figure unaffected by social class differentials in mortality indepen-dent of smoking. Comprehensive, consistent and reliable data for such an exercise are unfortunately not available. The data that are available however permit a limited but illustrative exercise to be undertaken. The data, especially for women, are far from complete, there being significant numbers of deaths for which information on last occupation, recorded at death registration, is inadequate to code social class, and it becomes increasingly unreliable at older ages.[19] For this reason only deaths under 65 are considered, and only for the largest causes of death. This was based on data for the period 1991-1993, for men and women aged 35-64 years and in respect of deaths from lung cancer, ischaemic heart disease and chronic obstructive lung disease.[20]

Percentages and numbers of deaths attributable to smoking by social class for each disease and for men and women were estimated in the same way as the UK figure. The total obtained by adding separate social class estimates was then compared with the estimate for all classes combined. In the case of lung cancer a second estimate by social class was produced. This subsumed different mortality risks of smoking for each social class, with US relative risks by educational level acting as a crude proxy for social class (Annex C).

Table 5.8   **Effect of estimating deaths by social class: 1991-1993**

							Number of deaths due to smoking**	
	Social class							
	I-II	IIIN	IIIM	IV-V	Total	Total†	Total	Total†
men								
Lung cancer	88	90	91	92	91	90	14,000	13,900
Lung cancer *	85	89	91	92	90	90	13,900	13,800
Ischaemic heart disease	39	43	47	49	45	44	22,400	22,000
Chronic obstructive lung disease	85	86	87	88	87	87	3,600	3,600
women								
Lung cancer	76	77	81	83	79	80	3,100	3,100
Lung cancer *	73	78	78	88	80	79	3,100	3,100
Ischaemic heart disease	35	35	41	46	40	40	2,300	2,300
Chronic obstructive lung disease	81	81	83	86	83	83	200	200

*Relative risks vary with social class, based on figures by educational grade from CPS II
**Numbers especially for women incomplete, provided as indicative only of differences
† Totals estimated directly disregarding social class

Social class gradients in the percentage of deaths caused by smoking reflect social class differentials in smoking (Figure 5.12, Table 5.8). The percentage of lung cancer deaths caused by smoking ranges from 88% for men aged 35-64 in social classes I-II to 92% of those in classes IV-V, or respectively 85% and 92% when different relative risks subsumed. For women aged 35-64 the figures range between 76% for classes I-II to 83% for classes IV-V, and with different relative risks from 73% to 88%.

With the exception of the first estimate of lung cancer deaths among women, summing the separate estimates of deaths by social class provides an estimate of deaths due to smoking which is slightly higher than or the same as that obtained for all classes combined. Numbers of deaths merely indicate the scale of the difference between the two estimates, absolute values being understated to the extent that social class cannot be ascertained, especially severe in the case of women. It may be seen that whilst differences in prevalence are considerable, the impact on estimates of deaths due to smoking are much less so.

In conclusion, the figures provide no evidence of significant bias in the UK estimate of deaths caused by smoking associated with social class differentials in cigarette smoking and mortality. If anything they suggest that the estimate derived for all classes combined slightly understates deaths from smoking.

Figure 5.12 **Separate social class and combined estimates of percentage of deaths due to smoking: England and Wales 1991-1993**

■ I+II ☐ IV+V
■ IIIN ■ Total
☐ IV+V ■ Total † (see table 5.8)

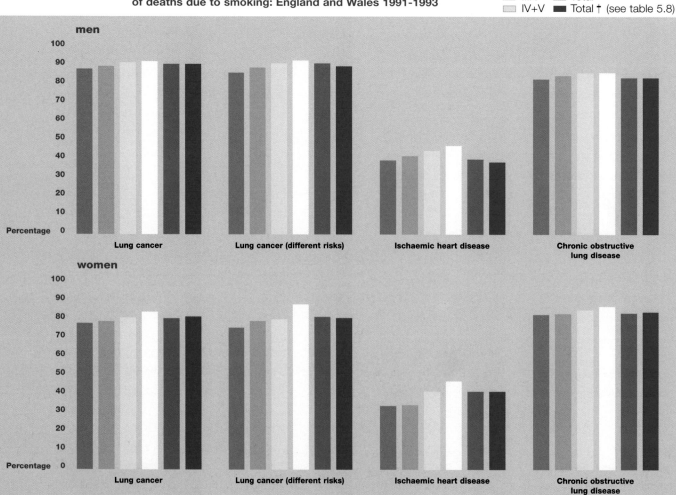

Comparison with other estimates of deaths caused by smoking

The current HEA estimate of the number of deaths due to smoking is greater than the earlier one in 1988 (110,000 deaths) because of the inclusion of additional diseases, based on evidence which has become available since the previous estimate was produced. The additional diseases, including those with a protective effect, account for an estimated extra 14,600 deaths caused by smoking.

The underlying trend in deaths of men caused by smoking in the period between the two estimates was downward, reflecting the downward trend in cigarette smoking in the past. Among women there remains a real increase, reflecting the upward trend in death rates from smoking between 1988 and 1995 in age groups of women aged 60 years or more. Deaths due to smoking from lung cancer for example, applying the present estimate of the percentage of deaths due to smoking, increased from 9,000 in 1988 to 9,500 in 1995 and from chronic obstructive lung disease by even more, from 7,400 to 9,300.

An alternative estimate for 1995 was produced using a different method by Peto and Lopez[16,21] The mortality risks of smoking used in the estimate were derived from the same study as the present estimate. The method however was designed for universal application, ruling out dependence on knowledge of smoking prevalence, or on quality of cause of death recording, and as a result included a broader list of diseases, all except cirrhosis and external causes. Lung cancer death rates for never smokers compared with lung cancer death rates in the population provided a reference for calculating deaths from other disease groups. Peto and Lopez estimate 131,000 deaths from smoking in 1995. This higher figure is mainly due to their higher estimate of deaths among women, 53,000 compared with 41,000, the figures for men being much closer, 78,000 compared with 80,000. The higher estimate for women is likely to be due to the longer list of diseases contained in Peto's estimate.

SUMMARY AND **OUTLOOK**

Recognising the present toll in loss of life illustrates the potential and the challenge for avoiding it in the future. Cigarette smoking killed 121,700 people in the UK in 1995, elevating the UK death rate by 23%. The 1995 death rate in the age group 35-64 years is an estimated 40% higher than it would have been in the absence of smoking. The impact is proportionately greater among men at present, the 35-64 UK death rate elevated by 50% on account of cigarette smoking, but the gap between men and women is narrowing.

These alarming figures do not exaggerate the impact of smoking, if anything they understate it. The estimate of deaths due to smoking is based on most recent evidence and consensus regarding the diseases that smoking can cause. It uses the best presently available data on mortality risks associated with smoking, demonstrated to be applicable to the UK in 1995. A cautious approach has been adopted, excluding diseases with a statistical relationship with smoking but for which the evidence is not yet established.

Consideration of the outlook is complex, requiring understanding of short and long-term mortality effects of past, present and likely future trends in cigarette smoking. To evaluate the mortality impact of present interventions it is necessary to distinguish between what can be expected in the short and longer term on the basis of present trends in cigarette smoking and what is amenable to change. The relatively long lead time to dying from smoking cigarettes calls for a vision of decades to come, for investment now to reap future mortality benefits.

Though complex, the wealth of available data about the UK smoking epidemic, covering trends in cigarette smoking and the mortality consequences, permits more informed analysis and projection to be undertaken than is the case for other behaviours and causes of death. The major challenge is not to anticipate future outcomes but to effect present change.

Men born around 1900, who would have started smoking around the first world war, were the first to smoke cigarettes from an early age, more than four in five of them becoming cigarette smokers, thus initiating the UK smoking epidemic among men. This was before the harmful effects of cigarette smoking were established, and, with no imperative to quit, smoking once started was generally for life.

The UK smoking epidemic among women started later, and peaked at a lower level than among men. Cigarette smoking reached a peak in the group born in the mid-1920s who would have started smoking in the early 1940s, three in five of them becoming cigarette smokers. Though the harmful effects of smoking were not generally known at the time, a post-second world war climate, evidenced by a slight fall in cigarette smoking among men, may have signified an arrest also in the increase in cigarette smoking among women.

Evidence of the harmful effects of cigarette smoking in the 1960s provided the impetus for smokers to quit smoking. Notable reductions in smoking during the 1970s and 1980s followed, especially among men, at whom the health education message was clearly targeted. Smoking behaviour changed radically, not only fewer young people starting to smoke but also, for those who did, patterns of giving up by age becoming established. Average tar yield of manufactured cigarettes fell during the period, though it is uncertain to what extent this was translated into an equivalent reduction in exposure to tar. A sharper decline in cigarette smoking among men than women during the 1970s and 1980s signified a convergence between the two. The smoking epidemics for men and women were moving into phase. Instead, social class became the key determinant of differentials in cigarette smoking.

A new phase of the smoking epidemic seems to be under way in the mid-1990s marking a halt in the decline in cigarette smoking and with signs of refuelling projecting a future increase. More young people are being recruited overall, and an earlier start among girls than boys means higher smoking levels among girls and young women. Quitting levels appear to be levelling off, if not falling. In middle and older ages women are as likely, if not more likely to smoke, as men. They are less likely than men to want to quit, to have tried to quit or to have succeeded in quitting smoking. Cigarette smoking for women appears to be influenced to a greater extent than for men by factors other than their own immediate health risks, lower smoking levels than men and higher tendency to quit in the 20s and 30s suggesting family-related factors such as quitting associated with pregnancy or looking after infants and children. The extent to which this is temporary quitting, to be resumed later, is yet to be established. Men on the other hand seem to more influenced by their own health risks, as evidenced by the higher quitting levels than women in middle and older age.

The impact of the smoking epidemic on UK mortality is profound and highly visible. Present death rates from smoking have their roots in past smoking behaviour, and can be linked directly to the paths of the smoking epidemic for men and women. Death rates from smoking peaked among the cohorts at the peak of the smoking epidemic, men born around 1900 and women born in the mid-1920s. In 1995, death rates from smoking for men had peaked and were falling in all age groups whilst for women death rates were still rising in age groups 70 years or more. Death rates from smoking among women aged 70-74 years are projected to peak by the year 2000 and in older age groups thereafter.

Continuing reductions in death rates from smoking are projected especially as 1970s and 1980s reductions in cigarette smoking, reflecting the massive impact of the health education message delivered in past decades, take effect. Present smoking trends however project a reversal some decades hence of the decline in death rates from smoking.

The closing of the gap between men's and women's cigarette smoking signifies a closing in future of the gap in death rates from smoking. At the same time social class differentials in mortality are projected to intensify on account of the earlier widening social class differentials in smoking. People who die from smoking are projected on present trends to disproportionately include women, and those in disadvantaged socioeconomic groups, men and women.

The UK smoking epidemic has had a major structural impact on overall patterns of UK mortality, to such an extent that it has reduced the female advantage in life expectancy. It is already visible in death rates for cohorts at the start of the respective epidemics for men and women, even though cigarette smoking levels were significantly higher for men than women. The coming together of smoking rates for men and women during the 1970s and 1980s is expected further to reduce it. The structural impact in coming years of social class differentials in smoking on patterns of UK mortality is expected to be equally profound.

The projected numbers of deaths do not only depend on death rates. The cohort of women experiencing the highest death rates from smoking were born during a period when birth rates were falling, and the expected increase in number of deaths not as large as the projected increase in death rates might suggest. By contrast the post-second world war 'baby boom' will have an inflationary effect on numbers of deaths from smoking for men and women in coming decades even though death rates from smoking are falling.

The situation that has been outlined calls for urgent action. The almost inevitable decline in death rates from smoking in coming decades is mainly due to measures taken in the past. The levelling off in the proportions starting to smoke, however, and in the proportions quitting, denotes that death rates will stabilise. Indications of an increase in cigarette smoking furthermore, if sustained, mean that death rates will rise again in the future, though this may not be apparent until several decades hence.

The current phase of the smoking epidemic suggests that whilst knowledge is widespread the momentum of the message that smoking kills appears to have reached a plateau. To avoid the projected increase in deaths from smoking, action is needed to boost stabilising quitting rates and to halt the increase in young people starting to smoke.

Ideally the best but also the most challenging way to reduce smoking prevalence would be to discourage young people from smoking in the first place. A striking feature of cigarette smoking among young people is the speed with which dependency develops. Smoking is a habit taken up casually, to enhance in a variety of ways perceived social effectiveness or simply to experiment. As evidenced in the number of young smokers who want and try to quit, dependency is rapid and cigarettes soon perceived to be necessary to function properly. The increase in young people smoking means an ever-increasing pool of addicted smokers faced with living with the habit, the imperative and difficulties of quitting and present and future health consequences.

Many recent health promotion activities have had little impact on discouraging young people from smoking. Stressing the harmful effects of passive smoking or smoking in pregnancy and measures aimed at reducing smoking in public places have resonance in encouraging smokers to quit, but impinge little on the recruitment of young people to smoking. Promoting the benefits of quitting by stressing reversibility of the harmful effects of cigarette smoking may ironically have facilitated recruitment to smoking. Smoking has come to be perceived as a manageable risk, with postponement of quitting a viable option and little reason not to start smoking in the first place.

When it comes to boosting quitting levels, projected mortality trends identify women and those in disadvantaged socio-economic groups as particularly at risk. Women have been the targets for tobacco industry advertising and likewise have to be the target of health promotion activities, over and above those concerned with the effects of smoking in pregnancy or on young children. This applies to all women, irrespective of age or social class. Disadvantaged socio-economic groups likewise need to be the targets of efforts to persuade and support them to quit. The poorest groups, unemployed people, lone parents surviving on benefits, those burdened, trapped and threatened by their lack of resources, are the ones among whom smoking levels are presently highest and health promotion activities have rightly been targeted to support them in quitting. However the figures indicate the need also for more widespread action in order to prevent large-scale, unnecessary and avoidable deaths from smoking in future.

Boosting quitting rates on the basis of individual mortality risks calls for a difficult balancing act, reinforcing the benefits of quitting even at older ages without reducing the incentives at younger ages. Concentrating health promotion activities on other than the individual smoker's risk has to some extent circumvented this problem, but often with questionably lasting results. Women encouraged to quit smoking when they are pregnant for example lack a rationale for quitting in the longer term. Just as young girls may be more prone to smoke for other-oriented reasons, such as losing weight, they may be more prone to other-oriented reaons to quit. The danger is that this diminishes the importance of their own mortality risks and incentives to quit on that account, thus rendering them more at risk at older ages. It would seem time to redress the balance.

To conclude, the scale of the problem and difficulties in achieving change in the new phase of the smoking epidemic have been highlighted. At the same time, by projecting the future based on current trends and in the absence of additional intervention, it presents a huge and timely opportunity and challenge.

NOTES AND REFERENCES

1 Health Education Authority. *The smoking epidemic: counting the cost in England.* London: HEA, 1991.

2 Office for National Statistics General Household Surveys 1973-1996. Material from the General Household Surveys made available through the Office for National Statistics and the Data Archive has been used by permission of the Stationery Office.

3 *Smoking among secondary school children in 1996.* London: Office for National Statistics.

4 The figures for 16-19 year olds were collected in the household and 11-15 year olds were collected in school and cannot be compared directly; evidence from the Health Survey for England 1995 which collected data on smoking among 11-15 years olds suggests an understatement among young people when asked in the household about health behaviours, though it is also possible that the classroom environment encourages overstatement.

5 Health Education Monitoring Survey 1996 data. Health Education Authority. Unpublished.

6 Health and Lifestyles Survey 1993 data. Health Education Authority. Unpublished.

7 Bennett N *et al. Living in Britain: results from the 1994 General Household Survey.* London: HMSO.

8 Continuous Household Survey 1994, Northern Ireland Statistics and Research Agency was the source of Northern Ireland figures, others based on General Household Survey data.

9 Wald N and Nicolaides-Bouman A (eds.). *UK smoking statistics*, 2nd edn, Oxford: Oxford University Press, 1991. (Data prior to 1973).

10 The birth cohort data is based on combined 1973-1994 General Household Survey data, collated according to year of birth. To avoid understatement due to later age at starting smoking, under 25s are excluded from the calculations; respondents interviewed before they start smoking would artifically inflate the figure of never-smokers. Likewise to reduce the mortality selection effect at older ages, over 80s are excluded from the calculations; since smokers die earlier, never-smokers become increasingly over-represented with increasing age. Despite this, the figures remain affected by truncation by age; the first possible observation for someone born in 1900 would be when they were in their seventies, whilst the most recent observation for someone born in 1960 would be when they were in their thirties. The result is understatement especially for earlier cohorts.

11 Doll R, Darby S, Whitley E. Trends in smoking related diseases. In: Charlton J, Murphy, M (eds.) *The health of adult Britain.* London: Office for National Statistics,1997. Table 9.3 updated to 1995.

12 Charlton J, Murphy M. Monitoring health – data sources and methods. In: Charlton J, Murphy M (eds.) *The health of adult Britain.* London: Office for National Statistics,1997.

13 US Department of Health and Human Services. *The health benefits of smoking cessation.* A report of the Surgeon-General. Maryland: US Department of Health and Human Services, Public Health Service, Centers for Disease Control, Center for Chronic Disease Prevention and Health Promotion, Office on Smoking and Health. DHHS Publication No.(CDC) 90-8416, 1990.

14 Grundy EMD. Population review: (5) The population over 60. *Population Trends* 84. HMSO (1996).

15 US Department of Health and Human Services. *Reducing the health consequences of smoking: 25 years of progress.* A report of the Surgeon-General. Maryland: US Department of Health and Human Services, Public Health Service, Centers for Disease Control Office on Smoking and Health. DHHS Publication No.(CDC) 89-8411, 1989.

7

16 Peto R, Lopez AD, Boreham J, Thun M, Heath C.
Mortality from smoking in developed countries:1950-2000.
Oxford: Oxford University Press, 1994 - for smoothed never
smokers age-sex-specific lung cancer mortality rates.

17 Total UK registered deaths is the sum of the national
figures. It may be lower than other published figures in which
the combined England and Wales figures includes a third
category 'elsewhere'. These are people who are not residents
of England and Wales but who died in England and Wales.

18 Hattersley L. Expectation of life by social class. In:
Drever F, Whitehead M (eds) *Health Inequalities*. Decennial
Supplement. London: Office for National Statistics, 1997.

19 Drever F, Bunting JL. Patterns and trends in male
mortality. In: Drever F, Whitehead M (eds) *Health
Inequalities.* Decennial Supplement. London: Office for
National Statistics, 1997.

20 Data provided by Office for National Statistics.

21 Peto R. Personal communication

ANNEX A: 1973-1996 TABLES OF CIGARETTE **SMOKING BY AGE**

Table A1 Current cigarette smokers by age and sex: Great Britain 1973-1996

men	1973	1974	1975	1976	1978	1980	1982	1984	1986	1988	1990	1992	1994	1996
16-24	50	50	44	43	40	38	36	35	36	33	33	35	35	35
25-34	57	56	50	48	48	47	40	40	37	37	36	34	34	38
35-44	53	55	50	51	49	46	41	38	37	36	36	32	34	31
45-54	57	56	53	51	48	46	40	41	37	37	30	30	26	28
55-64	55	51	50	48	44	44	39	36	36	31	28	27	24	26
65-74	49	46	43	40	39	36	34	30	28	26	26	21	19	19
75+	35	31	32	27	30	26	26	24	19	17	14	15	14	10
women	1973	1974	1975	1976	1978	1980	1982	1984	1986	1988	1990	1992	1994	1996
16-24	47	44	41	40	38	36	35	34	35	33	36	32	34	34
25-34	48	47	47	43	42	44	37	36	35	35	34	34	30	34
35-44	46	47	44	44	42	43	37	37	34	36	33	29	28	29
45-54	52	52	49	49	43	43	39	36	34	34	31	30	28	30
55-64	41	41	41	39	38	40	37	35	35	32	29	27	24	25
65-74	26	26	24	24	26	25	23	25	23	24	22	22	20	23
75+	13	12	13	12	10	10	13	12	11	11	10	11	7	9

Table A2 Ever-cigarette smokers by age and sex: Great Britain 1973-1996

men	1973	1974	1975	1976	1978	1980	1982	1984	1986	1988	1990	1992	1994	1996
16-24	57	57	51	51	47	45	42	41	44	40	40	42	41	43
25-34	72	73	69	68	67	66	61	61	57	54	52	50	50	51
35-44	74	73	74	75	74	72	71	69	68	67	64	59	56	55
45-54	84	83	81	82	79	77	75	73	73	72	70	68	63	62
55-64	86	83	84	84	84	83	83	80	80	77	73	72	69	73
65-74	83	83	83	84	83	84	81	77	81	79	79	78	75	75
75+	70	75	70	72	77	72	73	76	77	76	70	75	73	70
women	1973	1974	1975	1976	1978	1980	1982	1984	1986	1988	1990	1992	1994	1996
16-24	54	51	48	47	45	43	42	42	43	40	43	40	42	42
25-34	57	58	58	55	56	57	52	52	52	50	48	49	45	47
35-44	55	56	56	55	55	56	52	55	55	56	52	50	48	47
45-54	64	65	62	61	58	57	57	51	51	54	51	53	50	52
55-64	53	54	55	56	57	60	59	59	58	55	52	51	47	49
65-74	36	37	36	39	43	45	44	47	48	50	51	54	52	52
75+	20	20	21	21	22	26	27	30	28	31	35	35	34	38

Table A3 Ever-cigarette smokers who have quit by age and sex: Great Britain 1973-1996

men	1973	1974	1975	1976	1978	1980	1982	1984	1986	1988	1990	1992	1994	1996
16-24	13	13	14	15	14	15	16	16	19	17	16	16	15	18
25-34	22	24	28	29	27	28	34	34	35	32	30	32	31	25
35-44	27	24	32	32	34	37	43	44	45	46	44	45	40	43
45-54	32	33	35	37	39	40	46	44	50	48	57	55	58	55
55-64	36	38	41	43	48	47	53	55	55	60	61	63	65	64
65-74	42	45	48	52	52	57	59	61	66	67	67	72	75	74
75+	51	59	55	63	61	64	65	68	75	78	79	80	81	86
women	1973	1974	1975	1976	1978	1980	1982	1984	1986	1988	1990	1992	1994	1996
16-24	12	14	14	15	15	16	17	18	19	17	17	19	20	19
25-34	17	19	19	22	25	23	29	30	32	31	29	31	32	27
35-44	16	16	20	21	24	24	28	33	38	37	37	43	42	38
45-54	19	20	21	20	26	24	31	29	33	37	39	43	44	43
55-64	23	24	25	29	33	33	37	41	39	42	45	47	50	48
65-74	29	31	35	38	40	45	48	48	52	52	56	59	62	57
75+	36	41	38	44	52	60	53	61	62	65	72	70	79	75

Source: General Household Survey

ANNEX B: **DISEASES** THAT SMOKING CAN CAUSE

Eligibility of a disease for inclusion in the previous HEA estimate of deaths due to smoking was based largely on two reviews of the evidence, provided by the US Surgeon-General and the International Agency for Research on Cancer.[1,2] More recent reviews recommend additions to the list of diseases.[3,4,5] These, supplemented by further consultation, guided the selection of diseases to be included in the present estimate.[6]

Wald and Hackshaw note that since the 1985 IARC review, 'new evidence has reinforced conclusions about the diseases judged at the time to be caused by smoking, and new evidence has also identified additional diseases caused by smoking'. Reviewing cancers caused by smoking Doll likewise notes new evidence since the 1985 IARC review which justifies inclusion of cancers of the stomach and myeloid leukaemia as diseases which smoking can cause.

The cancers that it is now recognised that smoking can cause include cancers of the lung, upper respiratory site, oesophagus, bladder, pancreas, stomach, kidney and myeloid leukaemia.

Cancer of unspecified primary site has been added since the last estimate. Since deaths from cancers that smoking can cause represent a large proportion of all deaths from cancer it follows that a reasonable proportion of deaths in this category are from cancers caused by smoking. The argument for inclusion is reinforced by a large increase in use of this category in Britain, believed to be mainly artefactual.[7] Since we cannot be confident however that allocation to this category and the composition of it according to 'correct' site are comparable between CPS II and 1995 UK registered deaths, it seems appropriate that not all such deaths be included in the calculations. Instead erring considerably on the side of caution and to some extent arbitrarily only a proportion have been included. The proportion included is the proportion of all cancer deaths with site identified which can be tobacco-related. This approach undoubtedly underestimates the number of deaths caused by smoking but was taken to avoid any charge of potential over-statement.

Circulatory diseases which have been added to ischaemic heart disease, cerebrovascular disease and aortic aneurysm are atherosclerosis and myocardial degeneration.

In the group of respiratory diseases, pneumonia has been added to chronic obstructive lung disease (chronic bronchitis and emphysema). Pneumonia, a general term for several kinds of inflammation of the lung rather than a specific disease, has been added because of the massive evidence that deaths from it are associated with smoking in a biologically plausible way and because it is medically understandable as developing from chronic bronchitis. The inclusion of pneumonia became numerically more significant following the introduction in 1993 of automated cause of death coding in England and Wales.[8] Between 1984 and 1992 a broad interpretation of a rule for coding underlying cause of death was applied; when one of eleven listed conditions, including bronchopneumonia and pneumonia unspecified, would have been the underlying cause of death and there was any major condition mentioned elsewhere, in part I or II of the death certificate, the major condition was to be selected whether a causal sequence could be presumed or not. Automated cause of death coding, based on the US system, represented a reversion to the international application of the rule, in which a causal sequence took greater precedence. In 1993 as a result registered death rates from pneumonia, which went down by more than a half in 1984, rose again to almost pre-1984 levels.

Among diseases of the digestive system, cigarette smoking can cause deaths from ulcer of the stomach and duodenum.

One disease, cancer of the cervix, has been deleted, the available evidence suggesting confounding, with excess mortality risk observed for smokers a result of the relationship between smoking and number of sexual partners, an established risk factor for cervical cancer.

Smoking has been shown to be protective in respect of deaths from Parkinson's disease and endometrial cancer, though the number of deaths prevented is minimal when compared with the number of deaths that smoking causes. These have however been included in order to represent net smoking mortality.

B

Notes and references

1 US Department of Health and Human Services. *Reducing the health consequences of smoking: 25 years of progress.* A report of the Surgeon-General. Maryland: US Department of Health and Human Services, Public Health Service, Centers for Disease Control Office on Smoking and Health. DHHS Publication No.(CDC) 89-8411, 1989.

2 International Agency for Research on Cancer. IARC Monographs on the Evaluation of the Carcinogenic Risk of Chemicals to Humans: Volume 38: *Tobacco smoking.* Lyon: IARC, 1986.

3 Wald NJ, Hackshaw AK. Cigarette smoking: an epidemiological overview. *British Medical Bulletin*: 'Tobacco and health' ed. Doll R, Crofton J 1996; **52**(1):3-11

4 Doll R. Cancers weakly related to smoking. *British Medical Bulletin*:'Tobacco and health' ed. Doll R, Crofton J 1996; **52**(1):35-49.

5 Doll, R. Personal communication.

6 Doll R., Peto R. Wald N. Personal communication.

7 Swerdlow A, Doll R, dos Santos Silva I. Time trends in cancer incidence and mortality in England and Wales. In: Charlton J, Murphy M (eds.) *The health of adult Britain.* London: Office for National Statistics,1997.

8 Rooney C, Devis T. Mortality trends by cause of death in England and Wales 1980-94: the impact of introducing automated cause coding and related changes in 1993. *Population Trends*, 86, HMSO (1996) 29-35.

ANNEX C: **RELATIVE RISKS**: SELECTION OF SOURCE

The calculation of relative risks requires disease-specific mortality rates for current, ex and never smokers. The relative risks in the study population should be applicable to UK mortality in 1995. Key to this is comparability in respect of timing and scale of the smoking epidemic. Ideally the source would be an ongoing study involving a representative sample of the UK population, large enough reliably to estimate mortality rates by sex and age. In practice, the aim is to identify a study population which is similar to the population of interest, and with relative risks which are arguably representative of and applicable to it.

Preferably therefore a contemporary British study would provide the mortality risks of smoking to be used in the estimation of deaths caused by smoking. The only large-scale study in this country is a 40-year follow-up, from 1951 to 1991, of male British doctors.[1] A main drawback is the absence of data for women, whose relative risks differ from those of men on account of differences in timing and scale of the epidemic. Even the risks for men are not applicable to the UK in 1995 as the study spanned a period in the epidemic of rising relative risks. A three-fold increase in the risks based on 1951-1971 and those based on 1971-1991 was recorded as those born around 1900, the earliest cohort for whom cigarette smoking was established from an early age, reached ages of higher mortality. The option of using the most recent data from the study is ruled out by sample size and age truncation effects. (Annex D, Table D3 compares relative risks used for the present estimate with those in the British doctors study.)

In the absence of a suitable British study, the US population provides the best available alternative; the US and UK have followed similar patterns in smoking behaviour, though the UK epidemic among men started earlier and among women started later than in the US. The study selected is the Cancer Prevention Study (CPS II) conducted by the American Cancer Society. This was a prospective study starting in 1982 of more than 1.2 million people across the United States.

It followed the earlier Cancer Prevention Study (CPS I), started in 1959, and it was undertaken on account of CPS I relative risks becoming increasingly unrepresentative with the course of the US smoking epidemic: current smokers' relative risks for all causes increased from 1.8 in CPS I to 2.3 in CPS II for men and from 1.2 to 1.9 for women.[2]

The CPS II relative risks represent the most timely and applicable to the UK population that are available. They are the best available, but nevertheless are based on 1980s data. It is possible that they understate relative risks for women in the 1990s, which were continuing to rise in the 1980s as cohorts with maximal exposure reached ages of higher mortality.

Though CPS II risks seem the most appropriate in respect of comparability between US and UK in stage of the smoking epidemic, further checks were made for comparability of smoking history or exposure between CPS II and the UK population.

Enrolment in the CPS II study was by family, whose eligibility was determined by there being at least one person aged 45 years or more. All family members aged 30 years or more were included in the study. The eligibility rules yielded a CPS II age structure under-representing younger and older ages. An age-stratified approach is used therefore in estimating relative risks. The method of enrolment meant that the study population under-represented Black and Hispanic populations, people who were illiterate, people who were ill and people living in institutions, and over-represented the more highly educated when compared with the US as a whole. Absolute mortality rates as a result were lower than those of the general population though this in itself should not invalidate relative risks.

Key in judging whether relative risks from a study are applicable to the population of interest is comparability in respect of amount of exposure, or in the past history of smoking. Exposure, and relative risk therefore, for current smokers varies in particular according to the number of years smoked and the number of cigarettes smoked.

Duration of smoking is determined by current age and age at which smoking began. Current age for men is usually the primary indicator of duration of smoking, there tending to be relatively little variation in the onset of smoking. There have however been changes over past decades in the age at which women commence smoking, a younger age at onset accompanying the notable increase in the proportion who ever become cigarette smokers.

Comparison of CPS II and the General Household Survey (GHS) 1994 data indicates that men in the CPS II sample started smoking around a year later on average than in Great Britain, denoting a difference in exposure by the same amount (Table C.1).[3] Comparison of CPS II with GHS 1988 data denotes a smaller difference for age groups 50 or more, with 1988 figures lying between those of CPS II and GHS 1994. The figures support comparability of CPS II and contemporary Great Britain figures, with longer exposure reflecting earlier age at commencement among younger cohorts. Shorter exposure in CPS II than in the UK population means some understatement of relative risks in applying them to the UK population.

Women in CPS II started smoking between one and a half and two years later than in GHS 1994, the figures for 1988 once more intermediate. Both demonstrate a similar pattern, steadily increasing with age. Application of CPS II relative risks to the UK would appear in this respect to be valid, with an earlier start in the UK denoting a downward bias.

The number of cigarettes smoked is also a key indicator of risk. The figures at first glance indicate notably higher consumption among smokers in CPS II than UK (Table C.2). The CPS II figures feature much greater rounding of figures than General Household Survey, in part due to differences in the questions asked. In CPS II, smokers were asked the number of cigarettes smoked a day. The General Household Survey asks average number of cigarettes smoked on weekdays and weekends, the two combined into a weighted daily sum. More importantly, evidence from a comparison of butt length indicates that in the US a smaller proportion of the cigarette is smoked than in the UK.[4] Hence the relative risks per cigarette smoked are likely to be less than in the UK, while the total risk per cigarette smoker may be the same because of the greater total number smoked.

To a lesser extent, tar yield per cigarette is associated with differential mortality risks in respect of deaths from lung cancer. There is little evidence of significant differences between CPS II and the UK. Ninety per cent of cigarette smokers in CPS II smoked filter cigarettes, compared with 87% in 1994 in the

Table C1	Mean age began smoking by age and sex, CPS II and Great Britain					
	men			women		
Age	CPS II 1982	GB 1994	GB 1988	CPS II 1982	GB 1994	GB 1988
35-39	17.2	16.4	16.3	18.3	16.7	17.4
40-49	17.4	16.6	16.7	19.2	17.8	18.7
50-59	17.4	16.7	17.0	20.4	18.6	20.0
60-69	17.6	16.4	16.9	21.8	19.6	20.8
70+	17.8	16.9	17.5	26.5	23.2	26.6

CPS II – Cancer Prevention Study 1982-1988   GB – General Household Survey, Great Britain

UK. Women in CPS II smoked lower tar cigarettes than men, as in the UK. Due to the ongoing reductions in tar yields and availability of lower tar cigarettes since the start of CPS II, direct comparisons of tar yield are not very informative.[5]

Relative risks for ex-smokers also are associated with the number of years smoked and the number of cigarettes smoked, but they depend crucially on years since quit, falling with time since quit. Ex-smokers in the UK had given up smoking more recently than their CPS II counterparts, 16 compared with 11% in the past five years for men and 21 compared with 18% women (Table C.3). This would suggest CPS II relative risks understate those experienced by ex-smokers in the UK, especially in view of their relating to smoking status measured at the start of the study. Again, the questions asked were different – GHS including pre-coded time since quit – last 6 months, 6 month-year, one year, 2-4, 5-9 , 10+ years whilst CPS asked for age when quit.

To sum up, the CPS II and UK populations were found to be comparable in respect of duration of smoking, based on the age of initiation – fairly stable among men but falling among women in younger age groups. CPS II smokers smoked more cigarettes a day than those in the UK, but this was moderated by the habit of smoking less of the cigarette in the US. Former smokers in the UK had quit more recently than those in CPS II. On balance it seemed exposure levels were sufficiently alike for CPS II relative risks to be applied to the UK.

Socioeconomic differentials in cigarette smoking have been increasing in recent decades in the US and UK. The socio-economic composition of never smokers is skewed toward the higher status groups compared with the general population and vice versa for current smokers. In calculating the relative risks in the study population, differential socioeconomic distributions for current smokers and never smokers may bias the estimate. The social class bias depends on the relative social class distributions of smokers and never smokers, weighted by the social class

relative mortality risks. A higher proportion of those experiencing the higher mortality risk could result in an overestimate of relative risk.

CPS II's unrepresentativeness of the population as a whole, being skewed toward the more educated, brings with it the advantage of greater homogenity than the population and greater comparabaility in composition of smokers and non-smokers, with arguably less impact on estimates of relative risk. This notwithstanding, the figures were examined directly to assess the extent of the differing social class composition, in this case measured as conventionally in the US by highest educational grade. Current and ex-smokers relative mortality risks for lung cancer and ischaemic heart disease by educational status are shown in Table C.4 and likewise educational status separately by smoking status in Table C.5. Relative risks of lung cancer vary by educational grade, higher in particular among those with less than high school education. This group in CPS II were less likely to have switched to low tar cigarettes which may have accounted in part for higher relative risks, lung cancer being the single disease caused by smoking for which low-tar is associated with reduced risk. Nevertheless, in testing the effect of using different relative risks to estimate deaths from smoking from separate estimates by social class (see p. 37) was found to produce a higher estimate than using total relative risk.

Table C2 Cigarettes smoked a day by age and sex, CPS II and GHS 1994

men		Number of cigarettes smoked per day percent							
		1-9	10	11-19	20	21-29	30	31-39	40+
35-44	CPS II	9	6	8	27	6	16	2	26
	GB 1994	14	8	27	25	12	4	4	5
45-54	CPS II	8	5	7	27	6	17	2	27
	GB 1994	13	8	21	28	12	6	4	8
55-64	CPS II	8	6	8	31	6	16	2	23
	GB 1994	18	9	26	24	10	6	2	5
65-74	CPS II	12	9	12	36	5	11	1	14
	GB 1994	29	13	25	25	5	0	2	2
75+	CPS II	23	13	14	32	3	7	1	7
	GB 1994	46	10	23	16	1	0	0	3
Total	CPS II	9	6	8	30	6	15	2	23
	GB 1994*	18	9	24	26	10	5	3	5

women		1-9	10	11-19	20	21-29	30	31-39	40+
35-44	CPS II	14	9	12	32	6	13	1	13
	GB 1994	23	12	30	19	10	3	1	3
45-54	CPS II	14	10	12	33	5	12	1	13
	GB 1994	17	13	30	24	10	4	0	2
55-64	CPS II	15	11	13	35	4	10	1	10
	GB 1994	23	11	30	26	4	3	1	2
65-74	CPS II	18	15	15	36	3	7	0	7
	GB 1994	29	20	29	13	5	3	1	0
75+	CPS II	25	17	14	32	2	5	0	4
	GB 1994	46	20	20	11	1	1	0	0
Total	CPS II	15	11	13	34	5	11	1	11
	GB 1994*	22	13	30	23	7	3	1	2

*Standardised to CPS II Age Structure
CPS II, Cancer Prevention Study 1982-1988
GB - General Household Survey, Great Britain
Percentages may not add up to 100 due to rounding

Table C3 Ex-regular cigarette smokers according to the time since they quit smoking
by age and sex, CPS II and GHS 1994

| | | Years since quit smoking cigarettes | | | | |
| | | percent | | | | |
men		**Under 1**	**1**	**2-4**	**5-9**	**10+**
35-44	CPS II	7	7	7	28	52
	GB 1994	8	5	17	20	50
45-54	CPS II	4	5	5	18	68
	GB 1994	4	4	9	14	69
55-64	CPS II	3	4	4	15	73
	GB 1994	5	4	7	14	69
65-74	CPS II	2	3	3	14	78
	GB 1994	3	3	6	9	78
75+	CPS II	1	2	2	10	85
	GB 1994	1	2	5	8	85
Total	CPS II	3	4	4	16	72
	GB 1994*	4	4	8	13	71
women		**Under 1**	**1**	**2-4**	**5-9**	**10+**
35-44	CPS II	4	5	13	19	58
	GB 1994	8	7	15	20	50
45-54	CPS II	4	4	11	15	67
	GB 1994	7	6	10	16	61
55-64	CPS II	3	4	11	15	67
	GB 1994	8	3	10	18	61
65-74	CPS II	2	3	10	15	69
	GB 1994	3	3	8	16	71
75+	CPS II	2	3	8	12	75
	GB 1994	4	2	5	12	76
Total	CPS II	3	4	11	15	67
	GB 1994*	6	4	11	17	61

*Standardised to CPS II Age Structure
CPS II, Cancer Prevention Study 1982-1988
GB - General Household Survey, Great Britain
Percentages may not add up to 100 due to rounding

| Table C4 | Smokers relative risks by education grade: CPS II,1982-1988 |

	Relative mortality risks				
	men			women	
	Current smokers	Ex-smokers		Current smokers	Ex-smokers
	Never smoked=1			Never smoked=1	
Lung cancer					
College graduate	19.4	7.1		11.8	3.6
Vocational/some college	23.6	9.1		13.7	4.8
High school graduate	24.7	9.7		11.2	4.7
Less than high school	23.8	10.7		17.3	7.3
Ischaemic heart disease					
College graduate	1.8	1.2		1.8	1.3
Vocational/some college	1.8	1.3		1.7	1.3
High school graduate	1.8	1.3		1.8	1.2
Less than high school	1.6	1.2		1.8	1.5
All causes					
College graduate	2.3	1.4		2.0	1.3
Vocational/some college	2.4	1.5		1.9	1.4
High school graduate	2.1	1.4		1.9	1.3
Less than high school	2.1	1.5		2.0	1.5

| Table C5 | Education grade relative risks by smoking status: CPS II,1982-1988 |

	Relative mortality risks					
	men			women		
	Never smokers	Current smokers	Ex-smokers	Never smokers	Current smokers	Ex-smokers
Lung cancer						
College graduate =1						
Vocational/some college	1.1	1.3	1.3	0.9	1.0	1.1
High school graduate	1.1	1.5	1.6	1.1	1.0	1.4
Less than high school	1.5	1.8	2.2	0.9	1.3	1.7
Ischaemic heart disease						
College graduate =1						
Vocational/some college	1.1	1.1	1.2	1.1	1.1	1.2
High school graduate	1.2	1.2	1.3	1.4	1.4	1.4
Less than high school	1.5	1.4	1.5	1.8	1.8	2.1
All causes						
College graduate =1						
Vocational/some college	1.1	1.2	1.2	1.1	1.0	1.1
High school graduate	1.3	1.2	1.3	1.2	1.2	1.3
Less than high school	1.5	1.4	1.6	1.4	1.4	1.7

C

Notes and references

1 Doll R, Peto R, Wheatley K, Gray R, Sutherland I. Mortality in relation to smoking: 40 years observations on male British doctors. *British Medical Journal* 1994; **309**: 901-911.

2 US Department of Health and Human Services. *Reducing the health consequences of smoking: 25 years of progress*. A report of the Surgeon-General. Maryland: US Department of Health and Human Services, Public Health Service, Centers for Disease Control Office on Smoking and Health. DHHS Publication No.(CDC) 89-8411, 1989.

3 CPS II data provided by American Cancer Society.

4 Doll R, Hill AB, Gray PG, Parr EA. Lung cancer mortality and the length of cigarette ends: an international comparison. *British Medical Journal* 1959; I: 322-325.

5 Stellman SD, Garfinkel L, Smoking in 1.2 million men and women. *Journal of National Cancer Institute* 1986; **76**:1058-1063.

ANNEX D: **RELATIVE RISKS**: ESTIMATION

The previous HEA estimate was based on the first four years, 1982-1986, of the Cancer Prevention Study II (CPS II), these being the only ones available at the time. For the present estimate years 3-6 inclusive (1984-1988) have been used, the first two years, in common with Peto *et al.* discounted on account of the established bias in short-term results of prospective studies; a tendency to exclude persons who are sick at the outset means lower mortality rates in the study than the general population, with the result that the effects of smoking are accentuated and relative risks elevated.[1] The disadvantage of excluding the first two years is that the measurements of exposure, obtained at the start, become less accurate with duration of follow-up. Current smokers who quit smoking during the course of the study, would be included in reported relative risks for 'current' smokers, leading to understatement of the actual risk. (Table D3 compares relative risks used for the present estimate with those based on the first six years of the study.)

For the period 1984-88, deaths subdivided by cause, sex and age in five-year age groups at the time of death were related to the person-years for those who in 1982 had never smoked regularly, those who were current smokers and those who were ex-smokers.

An age-standardised approach was required to estimate relative risks, and one which took account of the very small, or zero, deaths occurring in some cells, especially to never smokers. The Mantel-Haenszel pooling method, developed for incidence rate data was selected.[2] This assumes a uniform effect within the range for which it is calculated.

Relative risks for a range of age groupings were examined for evidence of an association with age. In the case of ischaemic heart disease and cerebrovascular disease relative risks displayed a clear gradient, falling as age increased and other causes took on relatively greater importance. Relative risks for pneumonia too displayed a tendency to fall with age. This was due in part to the large proportion of deaths at older ages certified to pneumonia which also had senile dementia and related disorders recorded. For pneumonia

therefore, current smokers' relative risks were divided into those under 65 and 65 and over. For other diseases, whilst there may have been some indication of a relationship with age, it was not consistent enough, perhaps on account of the small numbers of deaths, to warrant inclusion and an assumption of uniform relative risk was adopted. The pooling estimates were a weighted sum of five-year age groups, the open-ended age group being 85+.

Relative risks assumed for diseases for which smoking is protective were 0.5 for Parkinsonism, based on consistent results from a range of epidemiological studies, and 0.7 for endometrial cancer, based on years 1984-92 of CPS II.[3,4]

Relative risks for myocardial degeneration were not separately available, and instead the broader category of 'Other heart disease', ICD code 420-429, was used.

Relative risks and 95% confidence intervals are shown in Table D.1.

Comparisons with those based on the first six years of CPS II, 1982-88 and with the British doctors study are provided in Tables D.2 and D.3. The figures confirm, for reasons given earlier, the lower estimates overall for the years 3-6 compared with 1-6 of CPS II, and also higher risks than those from the British doctors study.

Notes and references

1 Peto R, Lopez AD, Boreham J, Thun M, Heath C. Mortality from tobacco in developed countries: indirect estimation from national vital statistics. *Lancet* 1992; **339**: 1268-78.

2 Rothman KJ. *Modern Epidemiology*. Boston/Toronto. Little, Brown, 1986.

3 Marmot M. Smoking and Parkinson's disease. In Wald NJ, Baron J. (eds) *Smoking and Hormone related disorders*. Oxford; Oxford University Press, 1990: 135-41.

4 Peto R. Personal communication.

Table D1a Relative mortality risks by disease for current and ex-cigarette smokers compared to never smokers: CPS 1984-88

men	Current cigarette smoker Relative risk	95% confidence interval lower	upper		Ex-cigarette smoker Relative risk	95% confdence interval lower	upper
Cancer							
Lung	26.6	21.0	33.6		8.2	6.5	10.4
Upper respiratory sites	10.6	6.0	18.7		3.0	1.6	5.5
Oesophagus	5.3	3.1	9.2		4.0	2.3	6.9
Bladder	2.9	1.9	4.4		2.1	1.4	3.0
Kidney	2.8	1.9	4.2		1.6	1.1	2.4
Stomach	2.1	1.4	3.2		1.6	1.1	2.3
Pancreas	2.2	1.7	2.8		1.1	0.8	1.4
Unspecified site	4.4	3.3	5.9		2.3	1.8	3.1
Myeloid leukaemia	1.4	0.8	2.3		1.3	0.8	2.0
Respiratory							
Chronic obstructive lung disease	14.1	10.3	19.3		8.4	6.4	11.2
Pneumonia 35-64	2.3	1.2	4.4	35+ ⎫	1.3	1.1	1.6
65+	1.9	1.4	2.6	⎭			
Circulatory							
Ischaemic heart disease 35-54	4.2	3.1	5.7		1.9	1.3	2.6
55-64	2.6	2.2	3.0		1.6	1.4	1.9
65-74	1.7	1.6	1.9		1.4	1.2	1.5
75+	1.4	1.2	1.6		1.1	1.0	1.2
Cerebrovascular disease 35-54	5.1	2.1	12.2	35-64 ⎫	1.1	0.7	1.7
55-64	2.8	1.9	4.3	⎭			
65-74	2.1	1.6	2.7	65 + ⎫	1.0	0.9	1.2
75+	1.4	1.1	1.8	⎭			
Aortic aneurysm	5.3	3.8	7.5		2.6	1.9	3.7
Myocardial degeneration	2.1	1.8	2.4		1.2	1.1	1.4
Atherosclerosis	1.9	1.0	3.4		1.1	0.7	1.9
Digestive							
Ulcer of stomach + duodenum	4.5	1.9	10.3		1.6	0.7	3.2

D

Table D1b Relative mortality risks by disease for current and ex-cigarette smokers compared to never smokers: CPS 1984-88

women		Current cigarette smoker			Ex-cigarette smoker		
		Relative risk	95% confidence interval		Relative risk	95% confdence interval	
			lower	upper		lower	upper
Cancer							
Lung		**13.6**	11.6	16.0	**4.1**	3.4	4.9
Upper respiratory sites		**6.1**	3.8	10.0	**1.5**	0.8	2.9
Oesophagus		**9.3**	4.7	18.3	**3.1**	1.4	6.7
Bladder		**1.6**	0.8	3.0	**1.5**	0.8	2.7
Kidney		**1.3**	0.9	2.0	**1.0**	0.6	1.6
Stomach		**1.2**	0.8	1.8	**1.3**	0.9	2.0
Pancreas		**2.3**	1.8	2.9	**1.5**	1.2	1.9
Unspecified site		**2.1**	1.7	2.6	**1.2**	0.9	1.6
Myeloid leukaemia		**1.2**	0.7	2.0	**1.3**	0.8	2.0
Respiratory							
Chronic obstructive lung disease		**14.0**	10.9	18.1	**8.6**	6.7	11.0
Pneumonia 35-64		**4.6**	2.4	8.6	35+ **1.1**	0.8	1.5
65+		**2.0**	1.4	2.7			
Circulatory							
Ischaemic heart disease	35-54	**5.2**	3.3	8.3	**2.9**	1.7	5.0
	55-64	**3.0**	2.5	3.7	**1.1**	0.9	1.5
	65-74	**2.1**	1.8	2.4	**1.2**	1.0	1.4
	75+	**1.4**	1.3	1.7	**1.1**	1.0	1.2
Cerebrovascular disease	35-54	**4.5**	2.4	8.5	35-64 **1.1**	0.7	1.7
	55-64	**3.2**	2.2	4.7			
	65-74	**3.0**	2.4	3.9	**1.6**	1.2	2.1
	75+	**1.2**	1.0	1.6	**1.0**	0.8	1.3
Aortic aneurysm		**8.2**	5.4	12.5	**1.6**	0.9	2.9
Myocardial degeneration		**1.7**	1.5	2.0	**1.2**	1.0	1.4
Atherosclerosis		**2.2**	1.2	4.0	**0.8**	0.4	1.7
Digestive							
Ulcer of stomach + duodenum		**6.4**	3.3	12.4	**1.4**	0.6	3.5

Table D2   Comparison of relative risks based on years 1982-1988 with years 1984-1988

	men				women			
	Current Smokers		Ex-Smokers		Current Smokers		Ex-Smokers	
	1982-88	1984-88	1982-88	1984-88	1982-88	1984-88	1982-88	1984-88
Cancer								
Lung	24.8	26.6	8.9	8.2	13.4	13.6	4.6	4.1
Upper respiratory sites	11.8	10.6	4.0	3.0	6.3	6.1	2.8	1.5
Oesophagus	5.9	5.3	4.4	4.0	8.4	9.3	2.9	3.1
Bladder	3.2	2.9	2.0	2.1	2.4	1.6	1.8	1.5
Kidney	2.5	2.8	1.7	1.6	1.4	1.3	1.1	1.0
Stomach	2.1	2.1	1.6	1.6	1.3	1.2	1.3	1.3
Pancreas	2.4	2.2	1.2	1.1	2.3	2.3	1.6	1.5
Unspecified site	4.4	4.4	2.5	2.3	2.2	2.1	1.3	1.2
Myeloid leukaemia	1.8	1.4	1.4	1.3	1.2	1.2	1.3	1.3
Respiratory								
Chronic obstructive lung disease	12.5	14.1	8.6	8.4	12.5	14.0	8.0	8.6
Pneumonia 35-64	2.5	2.3	35+} 1.4	1.3	4.3	4.6	35+} 1.1	1.1
65+	2.0	1.9			2.2	2.0		
Circulatory								
Ischaemic heart disease 35-54	4.2	4.2	2.0	1.9	5.3	5.2	2.6	2.9
55-64	2.5	2.6	1.6	1.6	2.8	3.0	1.1	1.1
65-74	1.8	1.7	1.3	1.4	2.1	2.1	1.2	1.2
75+	1.4	1.4	1.1	1.1	1.4	1.4	1.2	1.1
Cerebrovascular disease 35-54	4.4	5.1	35-64} 1.1	1.1	5.4	4.5	35-64} 1.3	1.1
55-64	3.1	2.8			3.7	3.2		
65-74	2.2	2.1	65+} 1.1	1.0	2.6	3.0	1.3	1.6
75+	1.6	1.4			1.3	1.2	1.0	1.0
Aortic aneurysm	6.4	5.3	3.1	2.6	8.1	8.2	2.3	1.6
Myocardial degeneration	2.1	2.1	1.3	1.2	1.8	1.7	1.2	1.2
Atherosclerosis	2.3	1.9	1.2	1.1	2.0	2.2	0.8	0.8
Digestive								
Ulcer of stomach + duodenum	5.4	4.5	1.8	1.6	5.5	6.4	1.4	1.4

D

Table D3   Comparison of CPS II and British doctors study relative risks

	Current smokers' relative risk		Ex-smokers' relative risk	
	CPSII	**British doctors**	**CPSII**	**British doctors**
	1984-88	**1951-91**	**1984-88**	**1951-91**
Cancer				
Lung	26.6	14.9	8.2	4.1
Upper respiratory sites	10.6	24.0	3.0	3.0
Oesophagus	5.3	7.5	4.0	4.8
Bladder	2.9	2.3	2.1	1.6
Kidney	2.8	1.4	1.6	1.2
Stomach	2.1	1.7	1.6	1.0
Pancreas	2.2	2.2	1.1	1.4
Myeloid leukaemia	1.4	1.8	1.3	2.0
Respiratory				
Chronic obstructive lung disease	14.1	12.7	8.4	5.7
Pneumonia	2.0	1.9	1.3	1.3
Circulatory				
Ischaemic heart disease	1.9	1.6	1.3	1.2
Cerebrovascular disease	2.0	1.3	1.0	1.0
Aortic aneurysm	5.3	4.1	2.6	2.2
Myocardial degeneration	2.1	2.0	1.2	1.4
Atherosclerosis	1.9	1.8	1.1	0.8
Digestive				
Ulcer of stomach + duodenum	4.5	3.0	1.6	1.5

ANNEX E: ESTIMATION OF PERCENTAGES OF **DEATHS** **BY DISEASE** DUE TO SMOKING

The method adopted by the US Surgeon-General to estimate US smoking attributable mortality, and in the previous HEA estimate, was used.[1] The approach assumes that there is no difference according to cigarette smoking status in exposure to other risk factors for the disease. Registered deaths for a disease therefore are assumed to be made up as follows:

Deaths of people who have never been smokers, exposed to never smokers' death rates

+

Deaths of ex-cigarette smokers, exposed to never smokers' death rates and an excess risk associated with their earlier smoking.

+

Deaths of current cigarette smokers, exposed to never smokers' death rates and an excess risk associated with their smoking.

Based on this assumed structure, a formula has been derived which allows the proportion of deaths from the disease due to smoking to be obtained from knowledge of the proportions of current and ex-smokers in the population and the relative risk of current and ex-smokers dying from the disease compared with never-smokers. Only those deaths of current or ex-smokers associated with the excess risk are included in the estimate of deaths due to smoking. The attributable proportion, a, for each disease is estimated from the following formula:

$$a = [p_c(r_c-1)+p_f(r_f-1)]/[1+p_c(r_c-1)+p_f(r_f-1)]$$

where

p_c = proportion who are current smokers

p_f = proportion who are former smokers

r_c = relative risk for current smokers compared with never smokers

r_f = relative risk for former smokers compared with never smokers

In the case of diseases for which smoking has a protective effect, application of the same formula (though current and former smokers can be combined into one exposure category of ever-smokers) yields a negative figure whose absolute value is the ratio of prevented cases to actual cases.

UK estimates of the proportions by age of current and former smokers were derived from the 1994/95 General Household Survey for Great Britain, and the 1994/95 Continuous Household Survey for Northern Ireland (Table E.1).[2,3] To obtain the UK estimates the two were combined in proportion to the 1995 mid-year populations by age.

Percentages due to smoking were estimated separately for 10-year age groups 35-44, 45-54, ..to 75+. The rationale for doing so was to avoid the effects of the different biases by age in respect of smokers and deaths; higher prevalence at younger ages and higher mortality at older ages serve to inflate the estimates based on 'average' all-age figures. (Table E.2)

Percentages of deaths caused by smoking in larger age groups, provided in the main text, were obtained by adding estimates of deaths by age group and dividing by total number of deaths from the disease.[4,5,6]

Table E1 — Percentages by age of current and ex-cigarette smokers, UK 1994

	Age group				
	35-44	45-54	55-64	65-74	75+
men					
Current smokers	34	27	24	19	14
Ex-smokers	23	37	45	55	59
women					
Current smokers	28	28	24	20	8
Ex-smokers	20	22	23	32	27

Table E2 Deaths caused by smoking as a percentage of all deaths from that disease by disease and age at death, UK 1995

			Age group		
men	**35-44**	**45-54**	**55-64**	**65-74**	**75+**
Cancer					
Lung	91	90	90	90	89
Upper respiratory sites	79	77	76	75	72
Oesophagus	68	69	71	71	70
Bladder	47	47	48	49	47
Kidney	43	42	42	41	39
Stomach	34	35	36	36	35
Pancreas	29	25	24	21	17
Unspecified site	27	34	37	37	31
Myeloid leukaemia	17	18	19	20	19
Respiratory					
Chronic obstructive lung disease	86	86	87	87	86
Pneumonia	33	31	31	26	24
Circulatory					
Ischaemic heart disease	56	54	40	26	11
Cerebrovascular disease	58	53	33	18	7
Aortic aneurysm	64	63	64	63	61
Myocardial degeneration	30	27	27	25	22
Atherosclerosis	25	22	21	19	16
Digestive					
Ulcer of stomach + duodenum	56	53	52	49	45
Diseases prevented by smoking					
Parkinson's disease	39	46	53	59	57
women	**35-44**	**45-54**	**55-64**	**65-74**	**75+**
Cancer					
Lung	81	81	79	78	65
Upper respiratory sites	61	61	57	54	36
Oesophagus	73	74	71	70	55
Bladder	20	21	20	21	15
Kidney	9	9	7	6	3
Stomach	10	11	11	12	9
Pancreas	31	32	30	29	20
Unspecified site	4	7	9	10	5
Myeloid leukaemia	10	11	10	12	9
Respiratory					
Chronic obstructive lung disease	84	84	83	83	76
Pneumonia	50	51	46	18	9
Circulatory					
Ischaemic heart disease	61	62	33	21	6
Cerebrovascular disease	50	50	35	37	3
Aortic aneurysm	68	68	65	62	43
Myocardial degeneration	19	20	18	17	10
Atherosclerosis	23	23	19	15	5
Digestive					
Ulcer of stomach + duodenum	62	62	58	55	36
Diseases prevented by smoking					
Parkinson's disease	32	34	31	35	22
Endometrial cancer	17	18	16	18	12

Notes and references

1 US Department of Health and Human Services. *Reducing the health consequences of smoking: 25 years of progress.* A report of the Surgeon-General. Maryland: US Department of Health and Human Services, Public Health Service, Centers for Disease Control Office on Smoking and Health. DHHS Publication No.(CDC) 89-8411, 1989.

2 General Household Survey Data 1994, Office for National Statistics.

3 Continuous Household Survey Data 1994, Northern Ireland Statistics and Research Agency.

4 England and Wales mortality statistics, Office for National Statistics.

5 Northern Ireland mortality statistics, General Register Office for Northern Ireland.

6 Scotland mortality statistics, General Register Office for Scotland.

ANNEX F: **LIFE TABLE** CONSTRUCTION

The construction of separate life tables for current smokers, ex-smokers and never smokers required the estimation of UK age-specific mortality rates for the three groups.

Age-specific mortality rates were calculated as the sum of age-specific mortality rates from diseases caused by smoking and age-specific mortality rates from all other diseases. The first component differs between current, ex and never smokers, while the second is assumed to be the same for each.

For each smoking attributable disease and within each five-year age and sex category the mortality rate for never smokers was estimated from the following:

$$m_n = m_t/[1+p_c(r_c-1)+p_f(r_f-1)]$$

where m_n is the disease-specific mortality rate for never smokers and m_t is the disease-specific rate for the population, which includes never, current and ex-cigarette smokers. p_c and p_f are respectively the proportions of current and former smokers in the age group, and r_c and r_f respectively the relative risks for current and former smokers of dying from the disease compared with never smokers.

For each smoking-attributable disease and within each age and sex group the mortality rate for current smokers was estimated by multiplying the never smokers' rate by the current smokers' relative risk. Likewise, the mortality rate for ex-smokers was estimated by multiplying the never smokers' rate by the ex-smokers' relative risk.

The age-specific death rates for never smokers were equal to the sum of the never smokers' death rates for each of the smoking attributable diseases plus the age-specific rates for all other diseases. Current smokers' death rates were the sum of current smokers' death rates from smoking attributable diseases and deaths from other diseases, and ex-smokers' death rates the sum of ex-smokers' death rates from smoking attributable diseases and deaths from other diseases.

Life tables by smoking status were constructed from the death rates by smoking status. (Table F.1)

The proportion of smokers who die from their smoking can be estimated from death rates and life tables for current and never smokers, assuming they continue to smoke and subject to current mortality rates. The proportion of deaths of smokers due to smoking in each five-year age group is estimated by comparison of current and never smokers' death rates. This proportion is applied to the life-table numbers out of an original 10,000 aged 35 who die within the five-year age group to provide the number who die as a result of their smoking. Added together over age, the number and proportion of smokers who die as a result of their smoking can be estimated.

ANNEX G: ESTIMATION OF YEARS OF **LIFE LOST**

Years of life lost with respect to a given age were derived from life tables for never-smokers and deaths by age caused by smoking. With age 65 as the yardstick for example, the method is as follows.

For ages 35, 40 .., the average number of years a smoker would be expected to live before age 65 was estimated by subtracting expectation of life at 35 etc. years from expectation of life at age 65. The average years of life under 65 lost for deaths in a five-year age group was calculated by averaging adjacent figures – in the case of deaths aged 55-59 for example, the average of the figures for ages 50 and 55. This figure multiplied by the number of deaths in the age group caused by smoking provides total years lost for deaths in the age group. Summing the figures by age group provides total years of life lost.

(Table F1) **Life tables according to smoking status: UK 1995**

	never smoker		ex-smoker		current smoker	
men age, x	l_x	e_x	l_x	e_x	l_x	e_x
35	10,000	44.2	10,000	41.0	10,000	36.9
40	9,942	39.2	9,936	36.0	9,919	31.9
45	9,863	34.3	9,843	31.1	9,786	27.0
50	9,753	29.4	9,699	26.2	9,552	22.1
55	9,586	24.5	9,466	21.4	9,145	17.4
60	9,299	19.8	9,060	16.8	8,531	13.0
65	8,831	15.3	8,378	12.4	7,500	9.0
70	8,038	11.1	7,310	8.5	6,090	5.6
75	6,856	7.3	5,806	5.2	4,268	3.0
80	5,304	4.3	4,128	2.7	2,589	1.3
85	3,433	2.1	2,334	1.1	1,121	0.4

	never smoker		ex-smoker		current smoker	
women age, x	l_x	e_x	l_x	e_x	l_x	e_x
35	10,000	47.2	10,000	45.4	10,000	41.2
40	9,964	42.2	9,962	40.4	9,953	36.2
45	9,906	37.3	9,898	35.4	9,869	31.3
50	9,818	32.3	9,797	30.5	9,729	26.4
55	9,681	27.5	9,633	25.7	9,491	21.6
60	9,466	22.7	9,383	20.9	9,097	16.9
65	9,134	18.0	8,982	16.3	8,424	12.6
70	8,587	13.6	8,292	12.0	7,407	8.6
75	7,735	9.5	7,238	8.1	5,922	5.3
80	6,482	6.0	5,851	4.8	4,329	2.7
85	4,656	3.2	3,958	2.4	2,411	1.0

l_x is the number of survivors to age x out of 10,000 at age 35

e_x is life expectancy at age x